PATRICK MARBER

Dealer's Choice
After Miss Julie
Closer

with an introduction by Richard Eyre
and a foreword by the author

Methuen Drama

METHUEN DRAMA CONTEMPORARY DRAMATISTS

Published by Methuen Drama 2004

3 5 7 9 10 8 6 4

First published in 2004 by
Methuen Publishing Limited

Methuen Drama
A&C Black Publishers Ltd
38 Soho Square
London W1D 3HB

Dealer's Choice first published 1995, revised edition 1996,
this revised edition 2004; *After Miss Julie* first published 1996,
revised edition 2003, this revised edition 2004; *Closer* first published
1997, reissued with new cover design 2003, this revised edition 2004

A CIP catalogue record for this book is available from the British Library

ISBN 978 0 413 77427 9

Typeset by SX Composing DTP, Rayleigh, Essex
Printed and bound in Great Britain by
MPG Books Ltd, Bodmin, Cornwall

Caution

Contents

Introduction

Patrick Marber has said that without me he wouldn't have become a playwright. This is a fiction. I no more made him a writer than the team of monks who left Lhasa to seek out the new Dalai Lama made a tiny baby into a spiritual leader. It was his destiny, just as it was Patrick's destiny to become a playwright.

When you run a theatre you depend on luck. It's not the sort of sympathetic magic that's invoked with wilful optimism on first nights; it's the luck of finding talented actors, directors, writers on your doorstep who are keen to have your support. It was part of my luck at the National Theatre to be on the spot when two remarkable plays by then unknown writers came into my hands.

The first was a play that I read when I should have been meeting President Havel in Prague at a performance of *King Lear* but was prevented by a snowfall that crippled London and paralysed Heathrow. I sat at home and read a vast play about the American Right, McCarthyism, Mormonism, Marxism, the Millennium, homosexuality, AIDS, God and angels: *Angels in America* by Tony Kushner. I knew halfway through the first page – a virtuoso monologue by the monstrous lawyer Roy Cohn – that I wanted to put the play on. It had wit, intellect, originality and the unmistakeable authority of a real writer's voice.

The second comet that flew in my direction was *Dealer's Choice*. I had been tipped off by the playwright Nicholas Wright, who worked alongside me at the National Theatre as an advisor on repertoire and at the NT's Studio as a roving consultant and amanuensis. He has perfect pitch as a talent-spotter so when he told me about a writer who was the 'real thing' I didn't have to be persuaded with a cattle prod to read the play.

I knew a little of Patrick Marber as a comic writer and performer on radio – *On The Hour* and *Knowing Me, Knowing You*, and TV – *The Day Today* and *The Alan Partridge Show*. The shows satirised the earnest self-righteousness of populist current affairs programmes and the nauseatingly vain, sycophantic, self-serving celebrity interviewers, spraying clichés over their interviewees like Grand Prix drivers with champagne. These days we've become inured to Alan Partridge; his satirical edge has been dulled by his real life counterparts who have seamlessly merged with their satirical models.

There have been two occasions when I've had to stop driving because of a radio programme. On the first occasion I was listening to Joan Jara, the English wife of the Chilean folk singer, Victor Jara, who was tortured and killed by the Pinochet government, describing how she had identified his body – walking along the long corridors and dressing rooms of the football stadium in Santiago looking at the faces of corpses on floors, benches and tables. His broken hands – he was a guitarist – were what she recognised first. Her unemphatically factual delivery was unbearably moving and I was blinded by tears. The second occasion was the first time I heard *Knowing Me, Knowing You* and laughed so much that I was a danger to myself and a threat to other drivers. Alan Partridge was – and is – one of the great comic creations; that his co-creator should want to write a play for the National Theatre Studio I found vastly flattering.

As a first-time playwright Patrick was hardly a stranger to dialogue and narrative. But sketch-writing, whether it's for TV or stand-up comedy, is a different discipline to writing plays. The sketch-writer has to start with an epigrammatic idea, sprint down a straight narrative track and cross the finish with a clinching punchline. The playwright, however, has to play a long game: be an expert at sleight of hand, juggle revelation against concealment, portray character through action rather than description, and keep an audience occupied in one place at one time. Which is why – as some television comedy writers and novelists have discovered – playwriting is as difficult as juggling china plates against the clock while riding a unicycle on a tightrope over a raging torrent.

You know with plays as you do with actors – and indeed directors and conductors – if the piece of work is in the hands of someone who knows what they're doing: the play or performance or production or concert has an assurance: someone is in charge. Orchestras can be inspired by some conductors and seem commonplace in the hands of others – 'the masters of the brilliant wave' as James Galway calls them – just as some directors can animate a cast of actors while others, no matter how articulate and intelligent, seem unable to do more than direct the onstage traffic. So it is with plays. If you have to read a lot of plays you become an unforgiving judge: if the dialogue becomes flabby and generalised, the narrative meanders, the characters are unfocused and the meanings opaque; in short, if the author is unable to bring his orchestra in on the beat, then you become as impatient as Madame Defarge.

I once made a film for TV with the actor Denholm Elliott. I asked him how he chose his roles. 'I open the script in the middle and if there's someone there that I think I'd like to have a drink with I read the thing from the beginning,' was his reply. It's a test that *Dealer's Choice* would have passed with ease. I knew from the opening page that this was the work of a writer who knew what he was doing. It was terse, funny and revealing and, like all good plays and unlike fiction, was as much about the spaces in between the lines as the lines themselves. As they say of racehorses, you could see the breeding: Mamet out of Pinter, trainer and jockey Marber. And, like Mamet, Patrick wasn't making judgements about his characters; they occupied the grey zone, neither virtuous nor malign, not noble but not terrible.

I read *Dealer's Choice* and saw it in a 'workshop' production at the NT Studio – the culmination of readings, improvisations and rehearsals directed by the author. Soon after seeing the play, I had a meeting with Patrick. I can't remember what I said to him. I probably pushed a row of adjectival barges out to sea: outstanding, funny, compelling, touching, skilful, mature. I may have been planning to suggest that we look for another director for the play, but I was – if not shrewd – opportunistic enough to recognise that if I had, Patrick would have politely withdrawn his play and taken it somewhere where they would let him direct it. He was, after all, a poker player.

I think at the time – 1994 – that Patrick was 30, though as a friend says of him, 'He's always been 39,' and there was something impressively grown up about him. At a distance you might read into his stocky but slouchy build that he was an ex-footballer with a faint resemblance to one of the Portuguese team in the '66 World Cup, but close up his face was altogether too quizzical and thoughtful for a sportsman. That he was watchful, cautious, wary and tough might have been expected in a poker player (albeit one who had to be bailed out by his father in his early twenties), but the paradoxes were unexpected: he could be both diffident and determined, he would mumble discursively yet be wholly lucid, he would oscillate between trust and suspicion.

He had – and still has – a reputation for being a benign curmudgeon, earned by his Eeyorish habit of dolefully bemoaning his misfortunes, but it's a protective scepticism that conceals tenderness and a real capacity for love and friendship. What's more, it's an insulation against being hurt. No one who met Patrick with his then constant companion, his West Highland terrier, Riley, could have made the mistake of equating this droll if sometimes mournful man with the solitary and unfulfilled characters of his first play. Which is, of course, why he's a real writer.

And he had – rare among his generation – a love of the theatre. I had the wrong impression that he'd been an usher at the National Theatre (a profession with an illustrious heritage: from David Hare to Colin Firth to Matthew Bourne) but no, he'd been brought by his parents. 'I was a child when I saw your *Guys and Dolls*,' he said. (Well, he was eighteen.) His frequent visits to the theatre had given him an encyclopaedic knowledge of theatre and sophisticated sense of technique in writing, acting, direction and design.

This is from my diary at the time:

4th February 1995. *Dealer's Choice* has started previewing. It's a marvellously enjoyable piece of work, not at all like a first play . . . Patrick's spent years looking at and thinking about theatre, but his TV training shows (virtuously) in his avoidance of long speeches. His Mum (who I encounter

round every corner: 'Hello, I'm Mrs Marber') took him to
the NT regularly as a child. He's exacting almost to a fault
and is frustrated that the actors are never quite accurate
enough for him. He finds it hard to trust them.

It's true about Patrick and actors – or was – but acting in a
West End production of David Mamet's *Speed-the-Plow* may
have made him more sympathetic to the sometimes almost
alchemical process by which good actors arrive at a good
performance. He can be exasperated when actors seem
confused or obstinate, or wilfully head down a blind alley in
their attempts to inhabit a character, demonstrating the
truism that the only truth about 'The Method' is that there
are as many methods as there are actors. To him it's so clear,
it's all there in the text: meaning, intention, rhythm, nuance,
pacing, pausing.

In this, as in other respects, he resembles David Mamet
who said: 'You can delineate the intention by correctly
delineating the rhythm of the speech.' Patrick's writing, like
Mamet's, asks of the actors that they follow the score and
perform it without the intrusion of 'personality'. Mamet
again: 'There is nothing we feel nothing about – ice cream,
Yugoslavia, coffee, religion – and we do not have to add
these feelings to a play. The author has already done that
through the truth of the writing, and if he has not, it is too
late.'

I commissioned another play from Patrick. It was to be for
the National's 900-seat Lyttelton theatre – an auditorium
that can swallow up productions like a Bermuda triangle. I
believe that he got quite far with it: a yuppie reading group
(reading *Middlemarch*) meet in a flat owned by one of them
(something in the City); a car alarm goes off; they go outside
to find a group of black youths trying to steal the car; they
make a citizens' arrest, dragging the boys back into the flat.
And then? It could have been a brilliant platform for a play
about class, race, education, culture and crime. But I got
Closer instead.

There are very few British plays (as opposed to plays in

English) about sex: *Twelfth Night*, *Measure for Measure*,
Midsummer Night's Dream, *Private Lives*, *Look Back In Anger*,
Rodney Ackland's *Absolute Hell*, David Hare's *Blue Room*,
Christopher Hampton's *Les Liaison Dangereuses*, Tom
Stoppard's *The Real Thing*. And . . . er? According to its
author *Closer* is about the 'shock of passion'. The shock of
sexual passion is twofold: that you are able to feel any
emotion so strongly and that pain is the inseparable partner
of desire and jealousy.

It was said of *Closer* that it was about 'sexual politics' but
it's a strength of the play that it's not. It's about sex. Politics
is about generalities whereas sex, unless it's pornography, is,
like art, all about specifics. *Closer* is extraordinarily specific
about the minutiae of sex and the geometry of relationships.
In the play, sex is tender, romantic, loving, casual, intense,
brutal, selfish, squalid, savage; a blessing and a curse. It's the
underscoring of each life. 'Why is the sex so important?' is
the agonised cry of Anna to her partner when they're
confessing their mutual infidelities. 'BECAUSE I'M A
FUCKING CAVEMAN,' screams Larry, the mild
dermatologist.

The prurient would enquire what *Closer* had been 'based
on' as if all art were disguised memoir. It's based on life and I
doubt if there was anyone who saw this play, young or old,
gay or straight, man or woman, who didn't recognise its
observations with painful and guilty recognition. The radical
claim of its author – as far as the theatre is concerned – is
that any play about a relationship is a lie if it doesn't
encompass the sexual side.

Patrick told me of two women in their late sixties coming
out of the auditorium in the interval of a preview of *Closer*,
the last lines of the act still ringing in their ears:

Larry   You like his cock.
Anna   I love it.
Larry   You like him coming in your face.
Anna   Yes.
Larry   What does it taste like?
Anna   It tastes like you but sweeter.

Larry   That's the spirit. Thank you. Thank you for your honesty. Now fuck off and die. You fucked up slag.

Said the woman ruefully to her friend: 'I must have missed out on a lot in my youth.'

It was said of *Closer* that the play had echoes of Strindberg, but it's more that Strindberg had leaked into *Closer*, because with some prescience, shortly after *Dealer's Choice* had opened, Simon Curtis and Michael Hastings asked Patrick to do an adaptation for BBC TV of a nineteenth-century play about sex and class and the pain of living together, living apart and just plain living: *Miss Julie*. The third play in this collection is *After Miss Julie*: Marber after Strindberg.

In general, updating classics can be a minefield and a shift of period often seems to be no more than a meretricious fashion choice: is it to be Schiaparelli or Dior, Edwardian frocks or Sixties miniskirts? Occasionally a shift of period enhances the original, clarifying status and occupation and removing a layer of thick varnish. Sometimes a really unexpected harmony occurs between past and present and such is Patrick's version of *Miss Julie*.

The play is often revived in 'star' revivals – posh actress gets down and dirty with working-class actor – and almost invariably it lives down to expectations: audiences go expecting fireworks and find candles on a birthday cake. Moving the action from Sweden of 1888 to England of 1945 solved several problems in this notoriously difficult play.

First, the action of the original is set on Midsummer Night, in Sweden the night in which darkness never falls, a night of carnival and sexual abandon when the world is turning upside down. Relocating the play to the July night of the Labour landslide victory (the setting of *Absolute Hell*) provided a brilliantly illuminating parallel which injected a sense of social and sexual liberation in a truthful and accessible context: Britain on the cusp of revolution. The signs of class distinction – speech and manners – become brilliantly clear, and the allure of the one class to another gathers a real sense of political as well as sexual momentum.

Second, the shift in period gives specific reference points for an English audience, enriched by our knowledge of the history of 1945 and the irony of living in another age ushered in with a Labour landslide. In addition there's the enjoyably familiar paradox of the owner of the house – a Labour peer – being an aristocrat whose class is threatened. And with the detail of the lonely girl being shuttled between her suicidal father and emancipated mother, Miss Julie's hysteria, which usually seems merely enervating, becomes engaging and plausible.

Thirdly, it eliminates another layer of distancing – that odd and unavoidable disjunction that comes of seeing foreign plays with foreign settings and names played with English dialogue, idiom and physical behaviour. And fourthly, Strindberg's electrifying but baggy play has been edited, shortened and reshaped to its advantage. What's more, another English dimension has been injected, one alien to the Swedish original: wit. It's a fine addition to the catalogue of plays written by the post-war generation of playwrights about the period before their birth. 'I have been unfaithful to the original,' says Patrick characteristically, 'but conscious that infidelity might be an act of love.'

To be a playwright as prodigiously successful – and young – as Patrick is enviable. What's hard is keeping going. A playwright has to endure the effect of living to please and pleasing to live, year after year after year, all the while avoiding the unenviable occupational hazards of putting the mind and the ego in jeopardy. I've no doubt that not only will Patrick survive, but that also his best work lies ahead of him.

Richard Eyre
April 2004

Foreword

From November 1993 through to December 1994, *Dealer's Choice* was developed at the National Theatre Studio in the form of rehearsed readings, improvisations and a small-scale production. Without the studio and the benign guidance of Sue Higginson, who ran it, the play would not exist. Nicholas Wright and Giles Croft, from the NT's literary department, also gave me great encouragement at the time – my thanks to them.

On 25 February 1994 I received a fax from Richard Eyre saying he wanted to present the play in the Cottesloe Theatre the following year. That fax is now framed in my office. It marks the happy day I began to think of myself as a playwright. The actors David Bark-Jones, Nigel Lindsay and Nicholas Day were present at the first sessions at the Studio right through to the original production at the National. The characters of Carl, Mugsy and Stephen owe a great deal to their inspiration.

Dealer's Choice opened in February 1995. A few months later, Simon Curtis, the producer of the BBC's *Performance* series asked me if I'd like to write and direct a play for TV. He sent me Strindberg's *Miss Julie* and suggested I might like to be quite 'free' with it. I was immediately excited by the possibilities and had a strong sense of what I might do with the play. This is rare for me. I tend to work slowly but this came quite quickly. I spent the summer of 1995 writing it and the autumn making it. I was greatly helped by Michael Robinson and Michael Hastings. The former prepared a literal translation from which I worked, the latter was my brilliant script-editor at the BBC. The original cast suggested new material and various cuts. My grateful thanks to them.

The play is not a translation of the original. Rather, it is a 'version' – with all the ambiguity that word might suggest. I was unfaithful to the original. But conscious that infidelity might be an act of love.

After Miss Julie was first broadcast in November 1995. Some years later Michael Grandage (who had seen it on

TV) asked me if he could direct it on stage. We worked on the script making a number of changes here and there. The stage premiere occurred eight years to the month after the play had been broadcast on TV. It was a great experience; the Donmar Warehouse was a perfect space for the play, Michael's production was superb, the actors likewise. My thanks to him and to them.

I began *Closer* in the summer of 1996. I suspect my work on *Miss Julie* had got me thinking about this sort of territory. The title is stolen from Joy Division's second album. I wanted something implying motion and something that wouldn't limit the possibilities of what the play might 'mean'. I'd have preferred a title of my own but once I'd fixated on 'Closer' I knew it was right for the play I'd written.

At the time of writing, the internet was still a fairly new-fangled thing, by no means known to all. Lapdance clubs did not exist in the UK and plays about 'relationships' were very unfashionable. I was nervous. I thought *Closer* might vaguely appeal to a 'coterie' audience and that the majority would find it at best obscure and at worst insane. When I handed the play to Richard Eyre in the winter of that year I could barely look him in the eye.

In December 1996 I spent two weeks back at the NT Studio working on the material with four terrific actors: Kate Beckinsale, Sally Dexter, Stephen Dillane and Mark Strong. They read the play to an invited audience just before Christmas. Much to my relief it was alive. And it seemed possible I might not get stoned in the streets for writing it. My thanks to them, the brilliant original cast and all the subsequent companies who helped me as I continued to rewrite in rehearsals and occasionally previews.

The first draft of *Dealer's Choice* was written in my old flat in Noel Road, Islington (a few doors down from Joe Orton's old place) and at my then office in Peter Street, Soho (now a brothel, I believe). Much of *After Miss Julie* was written in a nice hotel in Italy. The first draft of *Closer* was written in Tyrone Guthrie's old house in County Monaghan, Ireland. To be exact, it was written in Lady Guthrie's bedroom at a

desk facing a lake beyond a field in which the occasional
cow would chew the cud. None of which is at all important,
but it's the kind of trivia that interests me when I read
forewords.

Patrick Marber
April 2004

Dealer's Choice

This play is dedicated to my parents

Dealer's Choice was first presented in the Cottesloe auditorium of the Royal National Theatre, London, on 9 February, 1995. Subsequently, it transferred to the Vaudeville Theatre, presented by Michael Codron. The cast was as follows:

Mugsy	Nigel Lindsay
Sweeney	Ray Winstone
Stephen	Nicholas Day
Frankie	Phil Daniels
Carl	David Bark-Jones
Ash	Tom Georgeson

Directed by Patrick Marber
Designed by Bunny Christie
Lighting by Mick Hughes
Sound by Sue Patrick

The play was presented by the Royal National Theatre in association with the Oxford Playhouse for an international tour in 1996. The cast was as follows:

Mugsy	Kieron Forsyth
Sweeney	Steve Nicolson
Stephen	Nicholas Day
Frankie	Justin Salinger
Carl	Rick Warden
Ash	Ken Oxtoby

Directed by Patrick Marber
Designed by Bunny Christie
Lighting by Mick Hughes and David Boswell
Sound by Sue Patrick

Characters

Mugsy, *a waiter, thirties.*
Sweeney, *a chef, thirties.*
Stephen, *a restaurant owner, late forties.*
Frankie, *a waiter, thirties.*
Carl, *Stephen's son, twenties.*
Ash, *a poker player, fifties.*

Place
London, England.

Time
A Sunday night and Monday morning.

Setting
Acts One and Two occur in a kitchen and restaurant.
Act Three occurs in the basement of the same building.

Act One

Early evening.

Stephen *is sitting at a table in the restaurant, drawing.* **Sweeney** *is in the kitchen preparing food.*

Kitchen.

Enter **Mugsy**.

Mugsy   Evening, Sween.

Sweeney   All right, mate.

Mugsy   Hey, Sween, this bloke I know won the lottery.

Sweeney   Oh yeah?

Mugsy   Yeah, he lives on my street. Eight million quid!

Sweeney   Reckon he'll bung you a few?

Mugsy   Nahh, he's a stingy bastard. He's bought a Ferrari. Takes his trouty old mum out for a spin. 'Cept it's up on bricks now, kids nicked the wheels.

Beat.

What I could do with eight million quid . . .

Sweeney   Lose it?

Mugsy   Oh yeah? Call.

Mugsy *tosses a coin.*

Sweeney   Heads.

Mugsy *catches the coin and looks at it . . . heads.*

Mugsy   Bollocks.

He hands the coin to **Sweeney**.

Sweeney   Business as usual.

Mugsy   Here, Sween, what d'you think?

He shows **Sweeney** *his tie.*

Bought it today, thirty quid.

Sweeney It's very nice.

Mugsy Yeah?

Sweeney It's very beautiful.

Mugsy You taking the piss?

Sweeney *examines the label.*

Sweeney Ooh, rayon.

Mugsy What's rayon?

Sweeney Greek – for rip-off.

Mugsy They said it was silk. Is rayon made of silk?

Sweeney All the time.

Mugsy Good. Is Stephen in?

Sweeney Next door.

Mugsy I've got to have words. (*Pause.* **Mugsy** *looks at* **Sweeney**.) D'you want to know why?

Sweeney Not really.

Mugsy Yes you do, you've got a *tell*, it's in your eyes. You forget you're dealing with a master of the psychological nuance here. I can read you like the proverbial book.

Sweeney What 'proverbial' book is that then?

Mugsy The book of psychological nuance. You OK for tonight?

Beat.

Sweeney No, not playing.

Mugsy Hallo?

Sweeney Goodbye.

Mugsy   What do you mean?

Sweeney   I mean, I'm not playing tonight.

Mugsy   What do you mean, you're not playing?

Sweeney   Is this an exam? I mean, I'm – not – playing – poker – tonight.

Mugsy   But you've got to play, if you don't play we're four-handed, Stephen won't play four-handed, there'll be no game.

Sweeney   I can't play.

Mugsy   We know that.

Sweeney *laughs sarcastically*.

Mugsy   Why can't you play?

Beat.

Sweeney (*smiles*)   I'm seeing Louise.

Mugsy   You're seeing a dolly bird?

Sweeney   *Louise.*

Mugsy   Louise?

Sweeney   My kid, you prat.

Mugsy   I thought your missus wouldn't let you see her?

Sweeney   Well, I'm seeing her tomorrow, special dispensation.

Mugsy   Tomorrow's tomorrow, you can play tonight.

Sweeney   I haven't seen my kid for three months, you could at least *pretend* to be pleased.

Mugsy (*sarcastic*)   Hurrah.

Sweeney   One dark night some deaf, dumb and blind old hag will spawn *your* child. A stupid, snivelling, scrawny mini Mugsy – then you'll understand responsibility.

Mugsy   And what about your responsibility to poker?

Sweeney   My Louise is more important. I'm not turning up to see her with red eyes, knackered and stinking of booze.

Mugsy   Don't drink then.

Sweeney   I'm sorry if it spoils your evening but that's the way it is. Finito. End of story.

Mugsy   Yeah, cheers.

Beat.

Supposing you win? You could take her somewhere special with the money –

Sweeney   Mugsy –

Mugsy   Madame Tussaud's, the Chamber of Horrors –

Sweeney   Mugsy –

Mugsy   Medieval torture through the ages, kids love that.

Sweeney   SHE'S FIVE!

Pause.

Mugsy   Call.

Sweeney   Why d'you bother?

Mugsy   Just call.

Mugsy *tosses a coin.*

Sweeney   Tails.

Mugsy *looks at it. Tails.*

Mugsy   Bollocks.

He hands **Sweeney** *the coin.*

You seen Carl?

Sweeney   No.

Mugsy   He said he'd come in at six, he promised.

Sweeney   Mr Reliable made you a promise, did he?

Mugsy   He's all right.

Sweeney   He's a ponce.

Mugsy   He's not a ponce.

Sweeney   How much does he owe you?

Beat.

Mugsy   Five hundred.

Sweeney   Mug.

Beat.

Mugsy   I've scrubbed the debt anyway.

Sweeney   You done what?

Mugsy   Fair's fair, can't have debts . . . between partners.

Sweeney   What are you banging on about?

Mugsy   If you must know, I'm banging on about a restaurant mate. Me and Carl are going to open a restaurant. French. Maybe Italian. The point is it'll piss all over this place.

Sweeney   *You're* going to open a restaurant?

Mugsy   Yeah, why not?

Sweeney   'Chez Mugsy'?

Mugsy   Oh, very witty.

Sweeney   A restaurant with Carl?

Mugsy   Stephen dotes on him. He's addicted to him. He'll give us the money to get us started. And then, once we're up and running . . . we dump him.

Sweeney   Who, Stephen?

Mugsy   No, Carl, we dump Carl.

Sweeney   Your partner.

Mugsy   It's business!

Sweeney   Have you told Stephen about this?

Mugsy   No, I'm waiting for Carl to soften him up. Of course, if *you* were to express an interest, if *you* were to come and see the premises it might sway Stephen in our favour. I'm talking business, Sween, I'm cutting you in.

Sweeney   I'm OK here, Mugs.

Mugsy   Seize the day, grasp the nettle.

Sweeney   Yeah and get stung.

Mugsy   Don't you want to be your own boss?

Sweeney   And I'd be my own boss if I worked for you?

Mugsy   Exactly.

Sweeney   You nipple.

Pause.

So where is this 'restaurant'?

Mugsy   I knew you were interested!

Sweeney   I'm just making conversation.

Mugsy   Yeah, you're like the Invisible Man, completely transparent.

Sweeney   He wasn't transparent.

Mugsy   Course he was, he was invisible.

Sweeney   That's not the same as transparent.

Mugsy   The Invisible Man was invisible, you could see straight through him.

Sweeney   Clingfilm is transparent.

Mugsy   So?

Sweeney   The Invisible Man was not made of clingfilm.

Mugsy   Course he wasn't, he was made of . . . fuck all!

Beat.

Sweeney   So where is this 'restaurant'?

Mugsy   Mile End.

Sweeney   There aren't any restaurants in Mile End.

Mugsy   Exactly.

Sweeney   No one's got any money in Mile End, it's a shithole –

Mugsy   *Used* to be a shithole, now it's 'up and coming'.

Sweeney   Says who?

Mugsy   Local estate agents, all of them. I've done my research. They say it's highly desirable, desirable people are moving to Mile End in skip loads.

Sweeney   Where in Mile End?

Mugsy   Mile End Road.

Sweeney   It's virtually a motorway.

Mugsy   It's a busy main road (granted) but that's good, plenty of passing trade.

Sweeney   *Where* in the Mile End Road?

Beat.

Mugsy   First rule of business, Sween; money first, information later. The premises are in a secret location that I will not disclose until the ink upon the deal is dry.

Sweeney   You've lost the plot.

Mugsy   I *am* the plot. Look, the point is Stephen is more likely to lend us the money if you've had a look.

Sweeney   Rubbish.

Mugsy   It's true, he respects you.

Sweeney   He respects you too.

Mugsy   Does he?

Sweeney   Course he does.

Mugsy   You reckon?

Sweeney   Course.

Mugsy   I respect him.

Sweeney   He respects you.

Mugsy *ponders.*

Mugsy   Yeah . . . maybe I'll have a quick word with him now . . . sow the germ in his mind . . .

Sweeney   You do that, Mugs, good idea.

Mugsy   You'll see.

Sweeney   Well, go on then.

Mugsy   I'm going.

He has forgotten to remove his florescent cycle clip.

This is me going, mate, to make my fortune.

Sweeney   Off you go then.

Beat.

Mugsy   How long you been working here?

Sweeney   Same as you, seven years.

Mugsy   Long time . . . seven years . . . itchy. Long time to be in the same place.

Sweeney *exits.*

Mugsy   Some can stand the heat, others stay in the kitchen.

He takes out a coin.

Call!

Sweeney (*off*)   Heads!

Mugsy *tosses the coin.*

Sweeney (*off*)   Just leave it on the table.

Mugsy *looks at the coin.*

Mugsy   Bollocks.

He thinks and then puts the coin in his pocket. He exits into the

Restaurant.

Pause.

Mugsy   Evening, Stephen.

Stephen   Hallo, Mugsy. (*Seeing the tie.*) My God, what on earth is that?

Mugsy   New tie.

Stephen   I'm afraid you'll have to take it off, it'll frighten the customers.

He returns to his work. **Mugsy** *hovers, nervously.*

Everything all right?

Mugsy   Oh yes, couldn't be better.

Stephen   Good.

Mugsy   Has Carl been in?

Stephen   Carl?

Mugsy   Your son.

Stephen   I know who he is, Mugsy. No, why?

Mugsy   No reason.

Beat.

Stephen   Are you all right?

Mugsy   Oh yes, I'm very well.

Beat.

Are you?

Stephen   What?

Mugsy   All right.

Stephen   I'm fine, thanks.

Mugsy   Good, I'm glad.

Stephen   Good, so am I.

Beat.

I must say I do enjoy these little chats.

Beat.

Are you *sure* you're all right?

Mugsy   Yeah. No. Well, one thing . . . I've just been talking to Sweeney and he says he's seeing his kid tomorrow and he doesn't want to stay up late so he won't play tonight.

Stephen   Tomorrow's tomorrow, he can still play tonight.

Mugsy   This is unbelievable, this is the same conversation that I had with Sweeney just now! It's amazing, it's like we've got something between us . . . something . . . begins with an 'S' . . .

Stephen   Sexual chemistry?

Mugsy   No!

Stephen   Sympathy? Synergy? Synchronicity?

Mugsy   Yeah, that's it. That's what we've got.

Stephen   We've got that, have we?

Mugsy   Yeah, loads of it.

Stephen   By the way, will you help Sweeney out tonight, you know Tony's not here.

Mugsy   Yeah, where is he?

Stephen   Bolton.

Mugsy   Bolton? What's he doing there? Committing suicide!

Stephen   He's at his father's funeral.

Mugsy   Oh . . . what did he die of?

Stephen   He committed suicide.

Mugsy   God, why?

Stephen   Because he lived in Bolton.

Beat.

Of course he didn't, he had a heart attack.

Mugsy   Heart attack . . . it can do that the heart, can't it . . . attack.

Beat.

Was there much history of death in the family?

Stephen   Yes, it's been a recurrent problem.

Mugsy   Still, life goes on.

Stephen   You could start a new religion with profundities like that.

Mugsy   Yeah. I mean, no – no, I couldn't, don't have the time.

Stephen   The point is we're short-staffed tonight so give Sweeney a hand if he needs it.

Beat.

Mugsy   Stephen, can I have a word –

Stephen (*holding up his work*)   What do you think?

Mugsy   Nice, very nice.

Stephen   Do you think it works?

Mugsy   What is it?

Stephen   It's our new logo for the restaurant.

Mugsy   Very nice. So Carl hasn't been in then?

Stephen   No, Carl has not been in, he won't be in until midnight for the game. Have you got something to tell me . . . about you and Carl? Mugsy, you can talk to me, you know.

Mugsy   I know.

Stephen   So talk to me. Come on, I want the truth . . . are you pregnant?

Mugsy   Pregnant, very good.

Stephen   Well, I'll just have to wait. You've got me all in a tizzy.

Mugsy   Well, that's just it, isn't it, Stephen, you and I, we understand each other . . . we operate on the same level . . . the same circle . . . we're on the same level of circles . . . aren't we?

Stephen   Yes. And could you ask Sweeney to come in?

Mugsy   You'll never persuade him, he's dead set.

Stephen   Well, we'll see.

He goes back to his work. **Mugsy** *hovers.*

Bye.

Mugsy   Yep, bye.

Stephen   It's that way.

Mugsy   Stephen, there is something I'd like to talk to you –

Stephen (*pointing to his watch*)   Mugsy . . .

Mugsy   I'll be going then.

Stephen   And Mugsy . . .

Mugsy   What?

Stephen   Cycle clip.

Mugsy   Cycle clip.

Mugsy *exits into*

Kitchen.

Sweeney *enters as* **Mugsy** *returns.* **Mugsy** *puts on a different tie.*

Mugsy   A man of vision!

Sweeney   You told him?

Mugsy   We had words.

Sweeney   Did you tell him?

Mugsy   Our conversation covered a gamut of topics, restaurantering was but one of them.

Sweeney   So you didn't tell him.

Mugsy   No. He wants to see you.

Sweeney   You didn't tell him I wasn't playing?

Mugsy   Sorry, mate, he prised it out of me.

Sweeney   Cheers, now I get an earful.

Mugsy   Not if you play.

Mugsy *starts to read the paper.*

Sweeney   Oi, the floor needs a mop in there.

Mugsy   It's Frankie's turn. He's late. Probably shagging.

Sweeney   Jealous?

Mugsy   No.

Sweeney *laughs.*

Mugsy   No! Did he pull that blonde bird?

Sweeney   Never you mind.

Mugsy (*wistful*)   She was gorgeous, tits like the Hindenburg. Two Hindenburgs.

Sweeney   Mugsy. Evolve. Floor.

Mugsy   It's Frankie's turn, have a go at him, or don't you want to cos he's your boyfriend?

Sweeney   You're unbelievable –

Mugsy   Well, your missus leaves you –

Sweeney   She didn't leave me, it was mutual.

Mugsy   Yeah, your missus mutually left you, Frankie moves in, tongues will wag –

Sweeney   Tongues will be cut off. Mugsy, do us a favour, mop the floor.

Enter **Frankie**.

Frankie   Evening all.

Mugsy *and* **Sweeney**   All right, mate.

Frankie   Where's Genghis?

Sweeney   Next door, first snoop expected.

Mugsy   Here, Frankie, Sween says he's not playing tonight.

Frankie   I know, no problem.

Mugsy   There won't be a game if he doesn't play, we'll be four-handed.

Frankie   No we won't, there's me, you, Stephen, Carl –

Mugsy   And?

Frankie   Tony.

Mugsy (*triumphant*)   He's at his dad's funeral.

Frankie Fuck.

Mugsy Yeah, big fuck.

Sweeney Look on the bright side, boys, you're not gonna do your bollocks for another week.

Mugsy I haven't done 'em for quite a long time actually –

Frankie Not since the . . . since the . . .

Mugsy Don't –

Sweeney The –

Frankie The un –

Mugsy Don't –

Sweeney The unment –

Mugsy Don't –

Frankie The 'unmentionable'?

Mugsy Oi!

Beat.

So?

Frankie What?

Mugsy Did you score?

Frankie When?

Mugsy Last night.

Frankie Who?

Mugsy The blonde with the hair on table ten.

Frankie Never you mind.

Mugsy Go on, did you hit middle pin? Did you fill your straight? Did you flop the nuts?

Frankie 'Fraid not Mugsy . . . but I got a shag.

Mugsy You're disgusting, you're like a dog on heat.

Frankie Bitches go on heat, Mugsy.

Mugsy You should have a test, mate.

Frankie I passed my cycling proficiency.

Sweeney No you didn't.

Mugsy You won't be laughing when you find out you've got HIV. When you get paid back for all your filthiness, you're pox-ridden, you're a walking syringe –

Sweeney Not in front of the food, Mugs!

Mugsy Your cock is a needle full of death, mate.

Frankie You smooth talking bastard!

Sweeney Here Frankie, has The Mug told you about his 'pleasure dome'?

Mugsy What 'pleasure dome'?

Sweeney In Mile End.

Frankie What's this?

Mugsy Never you mind.

Sweeney Mugsy's going into the restaurant business.

Frankie Oh yeah? Any chance of a job?

Mugsy You must be joking.

Frankie I think I must.

Sweeney Mugs, tell him where it is.

Mugsy Mile End Road.

Frankie Nice and busy.

Mugsy Exactly, thank you.

Frankie Plenty of local violence, good for atmosphere.

Mugsy You can get stabbed anywhere, nowhere's safe.

Sweeney   The question is *where* is it in the Mile End Road?

Mugsy   Never you mind.

Sweeney   See, Frankie, that's the big *mystery*. No one must know the secret location of Mugsy's Masterplan for culinary domination.

Frankie   So we'll never know?

Sweeney   You will go to your grave not knowing.

Frankie *and* **Sweeney** (*weeping*)   Why won't he tell us? Please, Mugsy tell us where it is!

Mugsy   All right, all right! If you *must* know I'll tell you.

Beat.

Sweeney   Too late now, mate.

Frankie   You had your chance.

Mugsy   No, I *will* tell you but if you tell anyone else –

Frankie   What? What you gonna do about it, *Tiger*?

Mugsy   I'll sue you.

Frankie   Oh right, I won't tell a soul then, Scout's honour.

Mugsy   Sween?

Sweeney   Swear, Brownie's honour.

Mugsy   I'm serious.

Mugsy *illustrates with his tie.*

OK, this is the Mile End Road.

Sweeney   Where's London?

Mugsy   Mile End is in London.

Sweeney   Where's Central London?

Mugsy   It is Central London, it's ten minutes from the West End, it's 'conveniently located'. OK, you know the police station?

Frankie   Yep . . .

Mugsy   Walk up fifty yards, crappy little park on your right?

Sweeney   Yep . . .

Mugsy   Hospital on the left.

Frankie   Yep . . .

Mugsy   You know the public conveniences?

Sweeney   Yep . . .

Mugsy *points as if to rest his case. Pause.* **Mugsy** *points again.*

Sweeney   No . . . No . . . tell me it's not true, Mugsy . . . *no . . .*

Mugsy   What?

Sweeney   It's a wind-up.

Mugsy   It's a Business Opportunity Scheme, this bloke from the council says I can have them for a grand. It's a grand!

Sweeney   It's a toilet!

Mugsy   They're *enormous*! It's potential on a stick. Come and see then you'll understand.

Sweeney   I've got a toilet in my flat, it wins prizes, I don't need to see another one.

Mugsy   Yeah yeah, they laughed at the man who invented the wheel.

Sweeney   Who was that then?

Mugsy   I don't know, Mr Fucking Wheel!

Sweeney   Friend of Mr Fire, was he?

Mugsy   Yeah and Mr Toilet.

Sweeney *laughs.*

Mugsy   Yeah, ha ha ha, big joke. Yes, it's a toilet, who cares.

Sweeney   Certainly not lovers of haute cuisine, they travel the world looking for the elusive 'khazi cum restaurant'.

Beat.

Frankie   You say it's the one near the hospital?

Mugsy   Yes . . .

Frankie   I had a piss in there last week. It's very spacious.

Sweeney *continues laughing.*

Frankie   No, Sween. Give the man a chance.

Mugsy   Thank you, Frankie.

Frankie   Don't worry, mate, your secret's safe with us.

Mugsy   Thanks, Frank. I'm glad someone understands.

Frankie   Best of luck, Mugs.

Mugsy   Cheers. Vision, that's all you need.

Frankie   Well, you got to have a dream, haven't you?

Mugsy   Yes you have.

Frankie   And your dream is a toilet in the Mile End Road.

Mugsy   You're a wanker, Frankie.

Frankie   No I'm not, it's just I'm *jealous* of your visionary perception. See, when I walk past say . . . a graveyard . . . I can't see it as anything other than a graveyard. *You* see a graveyard and think . . . *casino*. That's the difference between us, Mugs, vision. (*To* **Sweeney**.) I'm going for a smoke.

Frankie *exits.*

Sweeney   What is this?

Mugsy   What?

Sweeney   This.

Mugsy   This what?

Sweeney   This . . . business.

Mugsy   This is me.

Sweeney   This isn't you.

Mugsy   Yes it is.

Beat.

Sweeney   Did you tell Stephen it was a toilet?

Mugsy   Not in so many words.

Sweeney   In *any* words?

Beat.

Be careful, Mugs.

Mugsy   They're a grand, Sween, a grand. If we play tonight I could win a grand easy.

Sweeney   Or lose it.

Restaurant.

Enter **Carl**.

Carl   Hi, Dad.

Stephen   Hallo, Carl. What are you doing here?

Carl   Came to see you.

Stephen   I'll get my cheque book . . .

Carl   I don't need money.

Stephen   Hallelujah.

Carl (*seeing logo*)   That's good.

Stephen   Thank you, it's our new logo, I'm rather proud of it.

Carl   Yeah, it's great. I've got a friend who could artwork that for you.

Stephen   It is artworked, this is it.

Carl   No, I mean do the layout so you can have it printed.

Stephen   This *is* the layout.

Carl   No, I mean . . . d'you want a drink?

Stephen   In other words, 'Can I have a drink, Dad?'

Carl   Yes.

Stephen   While you're there could you tell Sweeney I need a word.

Carl   Sure. Do you want one?

Stephen   No thanks.

Kitchen.

Enter **Carl** *who walks through and off.*

Carl   All right, lads.

Sweeney   All right, Carl.

Mugsy   Carl, Carl, have you told him?

Carl (*off*)   Not yet, I've only just got here.

Sweeney   You playing tonight, Carl?

Carl (*off*)   Yeah.

He emerges with beer bottle.

Sweeney, Dad wants a word when you've got a minute.

He is leaving. **Frankie** *enters.*

Sweeney   Carl, you got that ton you owe me?

Carl   You said Saturday.

Sweeney   Yeah and today's Sunday.

Carl   No, Saturday next week.

Sweeney   *This* week.

Frankie   You got my fifty?

Carl   What fifty?

Frankie   The fifty quid you owe me.

Carl   I don't owe you fifty, do I?

Frankie   No.

Carl   You just said –

Sweeney   Where is it?

Carl   We said next week.

Sweeney   I need it, Carl.

Beat.

Frankie   What you playing with tonight, Carl?

Carl   Money.

Sweeney   So give me some.

Carl   I haven't got it yet, Sween, I'm sorry.

Sweeney   Well, how are you going to play then?

Frankie   Daddy will provide.

Carl   I'm *owed* money.

Mugsy   Leave him alone, he's good for it.

Sweeney   From who?

Carl   Tony owes me three hundred.

Beat.

Frankie   He's not here.

Carl   What?

Sweeney   He's at a funeral.

Carl   Where?

Mugsy   Bolton.

Frankie (*helpfully*)   You could get a cab.

Carl   Who died?

Mugsy   His dad.

Carl   I'll get you your money, Sween, I promise. Trust me.

Sweeney   *Why?*

Carl   What?

Beat.

Sweeney   Why should I trust *you*?

Pause.

Mugsy   Carl, good luck.

Carl *exits into restaurant.*

Mugsy   Look, if you need it that badly I'll cover it.

Sweeney   Just mop the floor.

Mugsy *exits.*

Restaurant.

Stephen   So . . . how are you?

Carl   Very well.

Stephen   OK for the game?

Carl   Uh huh.

Stephen   Actually, there may not be one. We've got a problem with Sweeney, he's seeing his sprog tomorrow, says he won't play tonight.

Carl   I'm sure you can work on him.

Stephen   How's your mother?

Carl   She's fine.

Stephen   Does she let you call her 'mother' yet or do you still have to call her Claire? And how's the drop-out centre? Sorry, drop-in centre.

Carl   It's a Healing Centre, Dad, they're doing very well, they're nearly in profit.

Stephen   *Nearly?* Well, I'll be.

Carl   You were a hippy once.

Stephen   Yuh, once.

Beat.

So . . . what do you want?

Carl   I've got a proposition. You know the Mile End Road . . .

Stephen   Wasn't it Eliot's inspiration for *The Wasteland*?

Carl   It's great, it's got character.

Stephen   Ah.

Carl   What do you mean 'ah'?

Stephen   Isn't 'character' a euphemism for ugly?

Carl   Look, Mugsy wants to open a restaurant –

Stephen   He wants to what?!

Carl   And he wants me to be his partner.

Stephen   I've heard of the blind leading the blind but –

Carl   Please, Dad. He . . . we need some money, a quick loan, for an initial deposit on the premises –

Stephen   What 'premises'?

Carl   The . . . *place*, in the Mile End Road.

Stephen   What sort of money?

Beat.

Carl   Three thousand pounds.

Kitchen.

Frankie   Sween . . .

Sweeney   Before you start I'm not playing.

Frankie   I know, no problem.

Pause.

Sweeney   So . . . did you give it one or what?

Frankie   'It'?

Sweeney   Blonde bird, Table Ten, well-developed.

Beat.

Frankie   Nahh, she got a cab.

Sweeney   You bullshit merchant.

Sweeney *exits.*

Restaurant.

Stephen   Do you really want to open a restaurant?

Carl   Yes I do.

Pause.

Stephen   I thought you wanted to be a . . . 'do nothing', we've been through all this.

Carl   I can't deliver pizzas all my life.

Stephen   So when did this Damascan conversion occur?

Carl   Does it matter? I thought you'd be pleased. You could teach us. I mean, you're right, I have been . . . 'treading water'. Look, can you lend us the money?

Stephen   Carl, I can't lend you this money just like that.

Carl   You could.

Stephen   I'm sorry, it would be irresponsible, I can't just give you and Mugsy three thousand pounds . . . the man's a halfwit. He's still paying me off for the 'unmentionable' and he thinks –

Carl   He thought you might have faith in him – and *me* – he thought in his innocence you might actually *want* to invest in him –

Stephen   Invest in him? What, as a tax write-off? The man's a cretin.

Carl   He's not a cretin, Dad.

Stephen   He's a bloody idiot.

Carl   Fine. Just let him down gently, don't do a number on him.

Stephen   Has he got any idea what it costs to –

Carl   I'm sure he's got no idea.

Pause.

Stephen   Look, Carl, I'm sorry, I do appreciate your desire to . . . if you worked here and learnt the business properly then maybe –

Carl   There's no point, it's not going to happen so –

Stephen   No, I don't mean work *for* me, I mean work *with* me. I'd like that, Carl, I'd like to see you more than once a week for a game of cards.

Carl   I've worked here before, it doesn't work.

Kitchen.

Sweeney (*entering*)   D'you do the washing up?

Frankie   Sorry. I'll do it soon as I get home.

Sweeney   I'll be home first.

Pause.

How come you're so late?

Frankie   Never you mind.

Sweeney   How come you're so late?

Frankie   Been to the travel agent.

Sweeney   Oh yeah? Booking a dirty weekend – alone – what is it, 'Wanker's Package'?

Frankie   Never you mind.

Restaurant.

Stephen   But you're OK for tonight? You are OK for the game?

Carl   Not exactly, I've got a cashflow problem. Tony owes me money.

Stephen   Tony's not here.

Carl   I know.

Kitchen.

Frankie   So you're seeing Louise.

Sweeney   Yeah.

Frankie   That's good.

Sweeney   Yeah.

Frankie   What time?

Sweeney   Nine.

Frankie   Early.

Sweeney   Yeah, we're going to the zoo, Mugsy suggested the Chamber of Horrors.

Frankie   She's only six.

Sweeney   Five.

Beat.

Frankie   Yeah, but it's her birthday soon, isn't it?

Sweeney   Last month.

Restaurant.

Stephen   So . . . are you saying you want me to lend you the money for the game?

Carl   No I'm not, I haven't got the money so I won't play.

Stephen   I don't believe this, first Sweeney cries off, now you. I've been hosting poker games for the best part of twenty years, I've never had such trouble getting a game together.

Kitchen.

Frankie   So what time does the zoo open?

Sweeney   I dunno, ten? Eleven?

Frankie   Gonna spend all day there? I mean, kids get bored easy, don't they?

Restaurant.

Stephen   If you don't play how are you ever going to learn?

Carl   Learn what?

Stephen   Self-discipline.

Carl   Poker's got nothing to do with self-discipline. It's about guts, it's about risk, it's about passion –

Stephen   You're living in a fantasy world Carl, you're not the Cincinnati Kid.

Kitchen.

Frankie   Be a shame not to play.

Sweeney   Frank, don't guilt-trip me.

Restaurant.

Stephen   Carl, poker is all about discipline. The discipline of the game itself and the discipline of turning up here every Sunday night with a hundred pounds to play in the game.

Carl   It's not school.

Stephen   It *is* actually, it's a poker school.

Kitchen.

Sweeney   What is this? Don't you understand I've got no choice.

Frankie   Course you've got a choice. You can play cards *and* see your kid.

Sweeney   HER NAME'S LOUISE! I want to be awake when I see my daughter. I don't want to be sulking about some pot I lost when she's looking at the . . . penguins all excited.

Restaurant.

Stephen   Carl, I taught you everything you know about poker.

Carl   I do OK . . .

Stephen   What about last week? You played like a mug, you outmugged Mugsy which is saying something.

Kitchen.

Frankie   Do you want to play?

Sweeney   Course I want to play.

Frankie   So stop pretending to be 'el perfecto daddyo' and play.

Restaurant.

Carl   OK, last week I lost but usually, this year, I've been winning.

Stephen   I'm sorry, Carl, you're wrong. I log every game, remember? You're losing.

Kitchen.

Frankie   You scared of losing?

Sweeney   No.

Restaurant.

Carl   It depends where you take the log from.

Stephen   You're losing.

Kitchen.

Sweeney   Yeah, all right, I'm scared of losing. I've done a grand the last three weeks, supposing I do all my dough tonight and then I've got nothing to spend on Louise tomorrow?

Frankie   Stick fifty quid in your back pocket, don't touch it.

Sweeney   I haven't got the discipline.

Restaurant.

Stephen   You've got no discipline, you bet when you should check, you call when you should – you play like a girl.

Carl   Well, you taught me.

Kitchen.

Frankie   You taught me how to play.

Sweeney   That was at school, Frank, it was years ago.

Frankie   So?

Restaurant.

Stephen   Well, then either I taught you badly or maybe, Carl . . . you don't learn.

Kitchen.

Sweeney   So . . . now you're a better player than me, all right.

Restaurant.

Stephen   Carl, why can't you –

Carl   What, be like you?

Kitchen.

Frankie   Lost your bottle? Gone soft?

Sweeney   There's no shame in being scared.

Frankie   There is at a poker table.

Sweeney   We're not at a poker table!

Restaurant.

Stephen   You can't spend your whole life borrowing money.

Carl   If it's so important that I play I'll borrow the money off *mum*.

Stephen   Don't bring her into this.

A series of intercuts between the two rooms.

Frankie   Come on, Sween.

Stephen   This is about you and me.

Carl   I thought it was about poker.

Frankie   Come on, Sween.

Sweeney   Drop it, Frankie.

Stephen   Your mother –

Frankie   You wanker –

Stephen   When I was your age I was supporting a family . . .

Sweeney   Go fuck yourself!

Stephen   While your mother sat at home on her fat buddhist arse . . .

Frankie   Cunt!

Stephen   With a feeding bottle in one hand . . .

Sweeney   You're the cunt!

Stephen   And a joint in the other!

Carl   So fucking what!

Improvised row sequence at full volume lasting about twenty seconds until **Mugsy** *marches into the kitchen carrying a mop and bucket.*

Sweeney   FUCK OFF, MUGSY!

Mugsy *exits into restaurant.*

Stephen (*to* **Mugsy**)   Out!

Mugsy *exits back into kitchen.*

Sweeney   FUCK OFF, MUGSY!

Mugsy   I am fucking off!

Mugsy *fiddles with the mop trying to get it to stand up against a chair.*

Stephen   Come and sit down, Carl.

Carl   Don't shout at me.

Sweeney   WELL, FUCK OFF THEN.

Carl   I don't have shouting, Dad.

Mugsy   This is me fucking off, all right.

Stephen DON'T BE SUCH A FUCKING LITTLE MADAM AND COME AND SIT HERE.

Carl No shouting.

Stephen (*shouting*) ALL RIGHT!

Sweeney FUCK OFF NOW!

Carl No shouting.

Mugsy I'm fucking off, I'm fucking off.

Sweeney SO FUCK OFF THEN!

Mugsy *exits*.

Stephen (*shouting*) All right, please just come and sit down and talk to me. Please, Carl, let's sit down and talk about this in a civilised fashion!

Pause.

Mugsy (*off*) I've fucked off!

Restaurant.

Stephen Look, you have to understand I can't keep lending you –

Carl But that's not it, Dad –

Stephen Will you just once, just *once*, let me finish a sentence!

Kitchen.

Sweeney I'm not playing, all right.

Frankie All right, you're not playing, fine.

Restaurant.

Carl Why does it have to be so emotional? Why can't it be like you're a bank and I'm a customer?

Stephen But, Carl –

Carl   So there's no emotional ties, so it's outside us, so it's just a transaction –

Stephen   How dare you, if you want money from a bank you go to a fucking bank.

Carl   I can't go to a bank.

Stephen   And why is that, Carl? Because you were a compulsive gambler. Because you were addicted to slot machines, which, by the way, is the most ridiculous thing I've ever heard in my entire life. No bank will touch you, Carl, because last year you were bouncing cheques all over London and your father, your father the bastard, i.e. me (by the way) covered all your debts so that you wouldn't go to prison.

Carl   I wouldn't have gone to prison.

Stephen   Yes you would. So don't call me a bank, don't for one second think there can be any 'transaction' between us that isn't emotional because whether you like it or not I am your father and you are my son.

Kitchen.

Frankie   D'you want a drink?

Sweeney   Yeah, go on, open a bottle of house red.

Frankie *exits.*

Restaurant.

Carl   Just because *you're* successful doesn't mean that I –

Stephen   *Successful?*

Carl   Yes you are, you've built this place up from nothing.

Stephen   Do me a favour, don't come in here spouting your naive olde worlde bollocks, 'Ee, Dad, you built this oop from nowt.' Who gives a fuck.

Pause.

(*Calm.*) I want you to play, Carl. If you don't play I don't see you.

Pause.

Don't you understand? It's blackmail.

Pause.

Carl   No it's not. Look, I haven't got the money so I won't play. See you next week.

Carl *walks to exit.*

Stephen   Here you are . . . one hundred pounds.

He holds up the cash. **Carl** *turns to exit.*

Please . . . Carl . . .

Silence.

Carl (*taking the money*)   I'm sorry.

Beat.

If I win tonight I'll pay it back tonight. OK?

Stephen   OK.

Carl   See you later.

Carl *exits.*

Silence.

Kitchen.

Frankie *returns with a bottle of red wine. He pours* **Sweeney** *a glass.*

Frankie   More tea, vicar?

Sweeney   Bless you, my son. (*Drinking.*) What's this?

Frankie   House red.

Sweeney   Bollocks, show me.

Frankie *shows him the label.*

Sweeney   Frankie, this is forty quid a bottle.

Frankie   The house has decided to drink *good* red tonight.

Sweeney   On your head, Frankie.

Frankie   Ooo, I'm so scared . . .

Pause.

Sweeney   Where's Mugsy?

Frankie   Downstairs, playing patience. He was cheating. Can't even win at patience.

Sweeney   I'm worried about him.

Frankie   Aren't we all.

Sweeney   No, I mean about his toilet.

Frankie   Chateau Mugs? Bottoms up.

Sweeney   He's serious, you know, I mean, Stephen ain't gonna give him no money.

Frankie   He won't give him a winkle.

Enter **Mugsy**.

Mugsy   Can I come in?

Frankie   You *are* in.

Mugsy   Yeah, but I mean, shall I go?

Sweeney   No, grab a chair and have a drink. I'm sorry. For shouting. I'm a cunt.

Mugsy   S'all right.

Frankie *begins to pour* **Mugsy** *a glass of wine.*

Frankie   Here you go.

Mugsy   No thanks, I've got to do the floor . . .

Frankie (*picking up the mop*)   I'll do it, Mugsy.

Mugsy   Are you sure?

Frankie   Yeah.

Mugsy   Cheers. (*To* **Frankie**.) Shall I try it now?

Frankie   Yeah, go on, have a go.

Frankie *exits into restaurant and begins to mop the floor.*

Mugsy   So . . . Frankie didn't persuade you to play?

Sweeney   'Fraid not, Mugsy.

Mugsy   Yeah, I'd be the same if I had a kid. Or I'd teach my kid to play, like Stephen did.

Beat.

It's a shame really 'cos tonight . . . was going to be my last game.

Sweeney   You what?

Mugsy   Yeah, I had a medical this afternoon and . . . the doctor says I can't play no more . . . I've got this rare heart condition . . . it can't stand the excitement . . . so that's it . . . no more poker . . . I've lost my greatest love . . . I'll get over it I s'pose . . . in time.

He sobs.

Sween?

Beat.

Sweeney   Is that the best you can do?

Mugsy   Yeah, I think it is.

Sweeney   You doughnut!

Mugsy   Go on, Sween, play! Go on! Play for *me*, please, Sween, for *me*, play for me, *please*, Sween, *play*. I feel lucky tonight, I feel lucky for you tonight. *Play!*

Sweeney   All right, if it makes *you* happy, I'll play.

Mugsy   Good man!

Sweeney   For an hour.

Mugsy   Good man!

Enter **Stephen**.

Stephen   Sweeney, have any of my messenger boys asked you to come and see me?

Mugsy   It's all right, he's playing.

Stephen (*to* **Sweeney**)   Are you?

Sweeney   Yes.

Stephen   Excellent!

Mugsy   I used my unique persuasive powers and he crumbled instantaneously.

Stephen   Good for you.

Mugsy   So did Carl have a word with you?

Stephen   Yup.

Mugsy   And are you chomping at the proverbial bit?

Stephen   I'm positively tumescent, Mugsy, but can we discuss it later? We're opening.

Mugsy   We certainly can. Prior to the game we shall thrash out the deal and then I will castrate you.

Beat.

With my poker sword. (*To* **Sweeney**.) And you.

Sweeney   Oh yeah?

Mugsy *exits into restaurant.*

Stephen   Cycle clip!

Sweeney   Stephen, is it OK to take the lamb off, we've only got one left?

Stephen   Fine, sacrifice it.

Beat.

Sween, have you heard about Mugsy's 'scheme'?

Sweeney   Yeah, it's been mentioned.

Stephen   What the hell am I going to say to him? I can't possibly lend him any money.

Sweeney   I know. Tell him straight.

Beat.

Stephen   I'm glad you're playing, Sweeney.

Sweeney   Well, I couldn't let you down, boss.

Stephen (*showing him the logo*)   Hey, what do you think of this? New logo.

Sweeney *examines it.*

Sweeney   Nahh, don't like it.

Sweeney *exits.* **Stephen** *exits into*

Restaurant.

Stephen   Gentlemen, to work. Frankie, fix the wobble under that table, will you.

Frankie   Yeah.

Stephen   'Yes' is the word.

Frankie   *Yes.*

Mugsy   There'll be no wobbly tables in my place.

Stephen   No, just wobbly waiters. (*Showing logo.*) Frankie, what do *you* think of –

Stephen *realises it's not worth it, he screws up his logo and throws it on the floor.*

Mugsy . . . rubbish.

Mugsy   Yes, boss.

Stephen   And Mugsy . . . cycle clip.

Mugsy   Yeah, cycle clip, cycle clip.

Mugsy *removes his cycle clip forgetting to pick up the rubbish.*

Stephen   Mugsy . . . *rubbish.*

Mugsy   Toss you for it.

Stephen   No!

Mugsy *clucks 'chicken'.*

Stephen   Oh . . . all right.

Mugsy *tosses a coin.*

Stephen   Heads.

Mugsy *looks at the coin.*

Mugsy   Yes! Tails it is! Go on, my son!

Stephen *picks up the rubbish.*

Mugsy   I told you, this is my night! The Mug Is On A Roll!

Act Two

Midnight.

*The restaurant is closed. One customer, **Ash**, remains seated at a table. **Stephen** and **Mugsy** are in the restaurant.*

Kitchen.

Frankie Another bottle?

Sweeney Yeah, why not.

*Exit **Frankie**.*

Restaurant.

Mugsy *approaches **Ash**'s table. **Stephen** exits into kitchen.*

Mugsy Would you like some coffee?

Ash Please. Cappuccino.

Mugsy Ah, no, sorry, the machine's broken. (*Shakes his head.*) Italian. We've got filter.

Ash I'll have filter.

Mugsy Filter, right you are.

Ash And a couple of Amaretti biscuits as well.

Mugsy I'm sorry?

Ash Amaretti biscuits. You know, with the paper, you burn them.

Mugsy You burn the biscuits?

Ash No, the paper. You set fire to the paper and it goes up.

Mugsy Why?

Beat.

Ash Physics.

Mugsy   Right, where would we be without physics? Probably upside down or floating. Actually, I meant why do you set fire to the paper?

Ash (*deadpan*)   For fun . . . it's fun.

Mugsy   I'll go and see if we've got any.

Mugsy *exits into*

Kitchen.

Stephen   Come on, Mugs.

Mugsy   It's not my fault.

Stephen   What does he want?

Mugsy   Coffee.

Stephen   Well, serve him his coffee and then with all the subtlety you can muster ask him if he wants his bill.

Mugsy   Why?

Stephen   Because I'd quite like to start a poker game this century.

Mugsy   It's rude to hurry people.

Stephen   Well, when you're running your establishment in the Mile End Road you can let your punters linger in the post-riot after-glow all night. Meanwhile, please get rid of him.

Stephen *goes back into the restaurant.*

Mugsy   Have we got any . . . of those biscuits that go on fire?

Sweeney *looks at him.*

Restaurant.

Stephen *approaches **Ash**'s table.*

Stephen   Everything all right?

Ash   Yeah, thanks.

Stephen   You enjoyed your meal?

Ash   Not really, no.

Stephen   I'm sorry, why was that?

Ash   My steak wasn't cooked and it was cold.

Stephen   Which steak did you order?

Beat.

Ash   Steak tartare.

They stare at each other.

Kitchen.

Frankie *returns with another bottle of wine.*

Frankie   More vino, Sweeno.

Sweeney   Cheers.

They drink.

So when you going on this holiday?

Frankie   Soon.

Sweeney   Who you going with?

Frankie   On me tod. I'm a big boy now.

Sweeney   I could do with a holiday . . .

Frankie   Better win tonight then, hadn't you?

Restaurant.

Stephen   Anything else we can get you before we close?

Ash   I asked for some Amaretti biscuits if you stretch to those.

Stephen   No, I'm afraid we don't. They're more of a 'trattoria' sort of thing I think you'll find. There's a reasonable one nearby I can recommend . . . if you're desperate.

Ash   I'm OK here, thanks.

Stephen   So you are. Good night.

Stephen *exits into the kitchen.*

Kitchen.

Stephen   Come on, Mugsy.

Mugsy (*off*)   I am coming on.

Stephen   Pour me a glass of that, Frankie.

Frankie *pours.*

Frankie   What's he doing in there?

Stephen   I think he's being snide about my restaurant.

Frankie   Must be from *The Good Food Guide*.

Sweeney   He weren't having a pop at my cooking, was he?

Stephen   No, he was having a 'pop' at me actually.

He drinks.

What's this?

Frankie   Wine.

Stephen   This is good claret.

Frankie   Table Four sent it back.

Stephen   Table Four were drinking mineral water all night.

Beat.

Frankie   That's why they sent it back.

Stephen   Show me the bottle. (**Frankie** *shows him the bottle but conceals the label*.) Frankie, show me the bottle.

Frankie *shows him the label.*

Stephen   The next time you want to steal a forty-pound bottle of wine you could at least have the decency to ask.

Frankie   Isn't that a contradiction in terms?

Stephen   Don't fuck around with me, this is theft.

Mugsy *enters with a cafetière.*

Frankie   I'll pay for it.

Stephen   You bet you will.

Frankie   Trade price by the way, no mark-up.

Stephen   You'll pay forty pounds for it.

Frankie *puts the other bottle on the table.*

Frankie   *Eighty.* Tell you what, why don't you knock it off my winnings tonight?

Stephen   It's not funny, Frankie.

Frankie   I'm not laughing.

Stephen   Neither am I.

Frankie   Well, I think we've established it's not funny then.

Stephen *rises.*

Sweeney   Girls, girls, girls! I told him he could have it, Stephen, take it out my wages.

Stephen   It's a touching gesture, Sweeney, but you're a pathetic liar. (*To* **Mugsy**.) GET A MOVE ON.

Stephen *exits.* **Mugsy** *exits into restaurant.* **Frankie** *takes out a pack of cigarettes.* **Sweeney** *takes them from him.*

Sweeney   Come on.

Frankie *and* **Sweeney** *exit.*

Restaurant.

Mugsy *places a cafetière on* **Ash***'s table.*

Ash   Cheers.

Mugsy   I'm afraid we don't have any of those . . . biscuits.

Ash   No problem.

Mugsy   I've got a Snickers if you want!

Beat.

Ash   OK.

Mugsy   What?

Ash   I said OK. I'll have it.

Pause.

Mugsy   Right. I thought you'd say no . . .

Ash   Have you got one or not?

Mugsy   Yeah . . . but I've eaten half of it.

Beat.

Ash   Well, I'll have the other half.

Mugsy   Right, I'll just go and get it.

Ash   Sliced.

Mugsy   Eh?

Ash   I want it sliced . . . on a little side-plate.

Mugsy   Right . . .

Mugsy *exits into the kitchen and off.* **Ash** *takes out his mobile phone and makes a call.*

Ash   Hallo . . . yeah . . . I've been held up . . . half an hour . . . *yes*, I'll be there.

Mugsy *returns with a side-plate.*

Mugsy   One Snickers, sliced, on a little side-plate.

Ash   Thanks.

Mugsy   Is there anything else?

Ash   Why, am I keeping you up?

Mugsy   No, it's just that . . . actually, we've got a bit of a poker game starting downstairs and we can't start until –

Ash   Until I've pissed off.

Mugsy   No, no, you stay as long as you like. Really, I've got all night to take their money.

Beat.

So . . . shall I get the bill then?

Ash   Why, you paying?

Mugsy   No. Oh, you paying, very good. No, no I'm not. So shall I get the bill?

Pause. **Ash** *slowly stirs his coffee.*

Ash   Carl's paying.

Mugsy   Carl?

Ash   Yeah.

Mugsy   So you know Carl then?

Ash   Yeah, he's late.

Mugsy   Yeah, he's always late. How d'you know him?

Ash   I'm his father.

Pause.

Mugsy   But –

Ash   Don't be daft. Quiet tonight, how's this place doing?

Mugsy *goes to the bar and begins to prepare the bill.*

Mugsy   OK, could be better. It's the management really . . . and the location . . . and the food. It needs . . . vision.

Ash   So what are you playing tonight?

Mugsy   Poker.

Ash   I know, you said, I meant what stakes?

Mugsy   Depends, starts small gets big, depends who's doing 'em. I always say it's no fun unless it hurts.

Ash   You play with more than you can afford?

Mugsy   Yeah.

Ash   What's the ante?

Mugsy   Two from the dealer.

Ash   Live blind?

Mugsy   Uh huh.

Ash   Dealer's Choice?

Mugsy   Yep.

Ash   Pot limit?

Mugsy   It starts pot limit and then about four in the morning the losers demand no limit.

Ash   You play with wilds?

Mugsy   You bet we do.

Ash   So what's your game?

Mugsy   You name it; Hold'em, Omaha, Irish, Lowball, Fiery Cross, Anaconda – I won't charge you for the Snickers.

Ash   You're spoiling me.

Mugsy   Chicago, Hedgehog, Mugsy's Nightmare –

Ash   What's that?

Mugsy   Mugsy's Nightmare? I invented that one; it's five-card stud, hi-lo, two down, three up, whores, fours and one-eyed jacks wild with a twist. The twist being I'm the only one who understands it.

Ash   Cards speak or declarations?

Mugsy   Either, it's dealer's choice.

Ash   Flushes count hi-lo?

Mugsy   Yep.

Ash   The wheel goes?

Mugsy   Everything goes. So you're a poker player then?

Ash   Me? No.

Carl enters.

Carl   Hi, Ash.

Ash   Hi, Carl.

Mugsy   Carl, Carl, how did it go?

Carl   What?

Mugsy   With Stephen. The restaurant.

Carl   Went well, Mugsy.

Mugsy   Yes! I'm about to see him to –

Carl   Hi, Ash, sorry I'm late.

Ash   No problem.

Carl   Good meal?

Ash   Terrific. Thank you.

Mugsy   The bill. Carl? This gentleman said you –

Carl   Yeah.

He gets his wallet out.

This is the famous Mugsy. Has he been serving you?

Ash   Yeah, very well, thank you.

Mugsy   Cheers. Twenty-nine pounds fifty, Carl.

Carl *gives* **Mugsy** *thirty pounds.*

Mugsy   Service?

Carl *gives him five pounds.*

Thank you, please come again.

Beat.

Do you want some more coffee?

Ash   No.

Mugsy   I'll . . . I'll go in here then.

Ash   Right.

Mugsy *exits into kitchen and off.*

Pause.

Carl   So how's it going?

Ash   Yeah, OK.

Pause.

Carl   Did you meet my father?

Ash   Yeah.

Carl   As I said? Anal or what?

Ash   He's OK.

Carl   Yeah, he's OK.

Pause.

Ash   Where is it?

Carl   I haven't got it . . . not all of it.

Ash   How much have you got?

Carl   Two hundred and sixty-five.

Pause.

Ash   You owe me *four grand*.

Beat.

Where is it?

Carl   It's . . . gone.

Ash   What do you mean it's 'gone'?

Carl   Casino, I've just been. I lost it. I mean, I had a
grand, really, I tried to win the other three playing
blackjack, the dealer was on a freak roll. I was playing
hundred quid a box . . . I was trying to count – like you
taught me . . . he was hitting aces and tens non-stop. Ash,
I'm sorry.

Beat.

Are you going to kill me?

Ash   Jesus, he thinks he's in a movie.

Beat. He stands up.

I told you it had to be tonight.

Carl   I know.

Ash   I've been telling you for three months you had to pay
it tonight.

Carl   I know.

Ash   I *owe* this money.

Carl   I know.

Ash   I have to go to a game *now* and pay this money.

Carl   I know.

Beat.

Ash   All right, fine. You said you could always get it off
your father. Go and get it off your father.

Carl   I'm sorry, I can't.

Ash   Listen *fuckbrain*, you go to your nice father now and
you tell him what a sad sorry little prick you are for
spunking all this money and you tell him the truth and you
promise him you'll never gamble again because you're a
fucking *loser* and you get me my money. *Now.*

Carl   And what if I can't?

Ash (*sarcastic*)   They'll come in here with big guns and blow
your brains out. BANG.

He hits **Carl**, *once. Hard.*

You fucking idiot. It's serious. It's a poker debt. It has to be
paid. You said, you *said* when I lent you this, this year, *all
this year*, you said your father was a soft touch, your father
the rich businessman with his swank fucking restaurant. You
said he'd give you the money if it came to it. Well, this is *it.*
Go crying, go begging, go suck his fucking cock I don't care,
just get the money.

Beat.

You want *me* to go in there and get it?

Carl   No, he doesn't know about the gambling. He thinks
I've stopped. I *can't* . . . it would kill him, he'd kill me. Ash, I
do love him, he's my father.

Ash   You think I care?

Carl   Yes. Come on . . . you like me.

Ash   Like is irrelevant.

Carl   *Please* . . .

Ash   Can't do it, Carl. This is fucked up. Get the money.

Carl   Please don't make me.

Ash   Right, I'll do it.

Ash *goes to enter kitchen.*

Carl   No, no, listen, why don't you play tonight? In our game, here, you'll clean up.

Ash   Clean up? In a baby's game? What do I win? A packet of Smarties.

Carl   There's money here, there's money, I promise. Mugsy lost three grand a month ago. Sometimes the game goes mental, everyone goes on tilt –

Ash   You think there's four grand here?

Carl   Maybe not four, three maybe –

Ash   I need *four*.

Carl   There's four, there's four. How much do you owe?

Ash   Ten.

Beat.

Carl   How much have you got?

Ash   Five, plus your fucking 'four'.

Carl (*close*)   Please. Come on . . . you're a professional . . . it's easy money . . .

Silence.

Ash   Who's playing?

Carl   Me, Mugsy, Sweeney – plays like a madman, can't pass, pure aggression, no brains. Dad, granite . . . just push the right buttons he's easy. And Frankie, he's quite good.

Ash   What does that mean?

Carl   He's a bit flash, likes to mix it up.

Ash   And he's quite good?

Carl   In *this* game, yeah. But you'll kill him. Please. Help.

Pause. **Ash** *looks at* **Carl***. Close.* **Ash** *takes out his mobile phone. He exits.* **Carl** *is left alone in the restaurant.*

Kitchen.

Enter **Sweeney** *and* **Frankie**. **Sweeney** *holding an airline ticket.*

Sweeney   So where you going?

Sweeney *reads the ticket, stunned.*

Frankie (*taking the ticket*)   Las Vegas, mate, the States. The US of A.

Sweeney   When?

Frankie   It's an open ticket, soon as I've saved enough money, couple of months.

Sweeney   To do what?

Frankie   Play poker.

Sweeney   *You*? Turn professional poker player?

Frankie   Yeah . . . why not?

Pause.

Sweeney   Because . . . but it doesn't mean you have to . . . what about . . . everything here?

Frankie   What 'here'?

Sweeney   Here . . . I dunno, me . . . Mugsy . . .

Frankie   You can come and visit me in my five-star suite at Caesar's Palace. (*Gangster.*) 'I'll lay on some broads.'

Pause.

Sweeney   I shouldn't play tonight.

Frankie   You said you'd play . . . I mean . . . don't play if you don't want to.

Sweeney   I don't want to let the boys down.

Frankie   Play for a while, see how it goes . . .

Sweeney   You want my money?

Frankie   No . . . Yeah.

Pause.

Sweeney   So how much you got saved, Frank?

Frankie   A few grand. One big win and I'm sorted. I'm going, Sween, there's no way I'm not going. I've got the ticket, one way. Business class. I've been saying for years I'm going to leave this shithole.

Sweeney   What shithole?

Frankie   This place, London, England, everywhere. This country's a shanty town. It's dead, Sween.

Sweeney   So go to Vegas.

Restaurant.

Ash *enters.*

Ash   You're lucky.

Carl   Thanks.

Ash   Three hours and that's it, I go to your father.

Carl   Thank you.

Ash   Why d'you piss me about?

Carl   I haven't done it on purpose.

Ash (*softly*)   What about all the meals at the casino? The money? The drinks, the late nights, the cabs. I've given you my time. I taught you how to play. I've covered your debts for a year. I *trusted* you . . . and you repay me like . . . you're compulsive.

Carl   And you're not?

Ash   No, only thing I'm addicted to is these. (*He holds up his cigarette.*)

Carl   Sorry, can I have one?

Ash   Fuck off. Get your own.

Carl   Come on, don't be like my dad.

Ash   I'm not like your dad, Carl – I don't care about you.

Pause.

Carl   I . . . thought you liked me?

Beat.

Ash   Not especially.

Pause.

Carl   Why do you . . . why did you let me play in your game?

Ash   The big boys' game?

Carl   Yes.

Ash   Cos you're a mug. You're value.

Pause.

Carl   So . . . if you don't *like* me, why don't you go to him now and get the money . . . what is this?

Ash   Pity.

Carl   You *pity* me?

Ash   No, your father.

Silence.

Carl   Who shall I say you are?

Ash   What do you mean?

Carl   I can't say, 'this is Ash, he's a professional poker player, is it OK if he sits down and takes your money'.

Ash   Say what you like, it's your problem.

Carl   You're my teacher, *ex*-teacher.

Ash   From where?

Carl   School.

Ash   What a mess.

Kitchen.

Enter **Mugsy**.

Mugsy   Seen Stephen?

Frankie   No.

Mugsy *exits into*

Restaurant.

Mugsy   Seen your dad?

Carl   No.

Mugsy (*to* **Ash**)   Sorry, everything OK?

Ash   Fine.

Carl   Mugs, do you reckon it'd be OK if Ash sat in with us tonight?

Mugsy   Dunno, better ask your dad. I thought you didn't play?

Ash   I play a bit, I'm learning.

Mugsy   Yeah, got to start somewhere. We'll teach you! (*To* **Carl**.) He must be downstairs setting up. Will you tell him I want words.

Carl   Yeah. (*To* **Ash**.) OK?

Ash   Smashing.

Carl *takes* **Mugsy** *to one side.*

Carl   Mugs, when you're talking to dad, don't mention the *figures*, talk generally. We've got to deal with him carefully, OK?

Mugsy   I think I know how to handle a business situation.

Carl   Just don't talk about the actual sums involved.

Mugsy   The grand?

Carl   Exactly. We might want more, start up capital, let's be flexible, eh?

Mugsy   Flexible, like it.

Carl *exits into*

Kitchen.

Sweeney   You got my money, Carl?

Carl   No.

Carl *exits.*

Sweeney   Here, Frankie, do us a favour, look after this?

Frankie   What . . .

He hands **Frankie** *some cash.*

Sweeney   Fifty quid. Don't let me touch it.

Frankie   OK.

Sweeney   I'm serious. Don't let me play with it.

Frankie   OK.

Restaurant.

Mugsy   So where did you say you knew Carl from?

Ash   I didn't say. I used to . . .

Mugsy   What?

Ash   No, nothing.

Mugsy   You were saying? You used to . . .

Ash   I used to be his teacher.

Mugsy   Oh right, what subject?

Beat.

Ash   Economics.

Mugsy   Economics, always useful. Money makes the world go round and all that. Here, you know in medieval times when they didn't know the earth was round, do you reckon they said 'Money makes the world go flat'?!

Ash   Yeah, probably.

Mugsy   So where did you teach Carl? He went to some boarding school, didn't he?

Ash   Yeah.

Mugsy   Personally I think it's cruel, packing your kids off to some place in the country full of poofs, no offence.

Ash   I don't teach any more.

Mugsy   Oh right, what d'you do now?

Ash   I'm in business.

Mugsy   What sort?

Ash   Investment.

Mugsy   Right. What *exactly* is investment? I mean, I know what investment is but what . . . what is it exactly?

Ash   Give it a fucking rest, will you?

Beat.

Mugsy   Sorry. I do go on a bit sometimes.

Mugsy *exits into*

Kitchen.

Mugsy   I don't believe it, I see it but I don't believe it!

Frankie   Caught your own reflection?

Mugsy   Carl just invited that bloke to play tonight.

Frankie   You what?

Mugsy   Serious. I've been sussing him out.

Frankie   Ooo, Sherlock Mugsy.

Mugsy   Listen, I've learnt all about him thus giving me the edge over you mugs.

Sweeney So what's he like, Miss Marple?

Mugsy Seems all right, bit weird.

Frankie Is he rich?

Mugsy Yeah, he's an investor.

Frankie In what?

Mugsy I dunno.

Frankie What does he look like?

Mugsy Like a bloke.

Frankie Does he look like a mug?

Mugsy I don't know!

Sweeney Using your powers of psychological nuance would you say he looks like a mug?

Mugsy I don't know, what does a mug look like?

Sweeney and **Frankie** *laugh*.

Frankie (*to* **Sweeney**) That means you don't have to play . . .

Sweeney I'll play, I'm all right.

Mugsy You wait till tonight. I shall roast you. I shall have your scrotums on a silver platter.

Frankie Delicacy of 'Mugsy's Mile End Bistro Shithouse'?

Mugsy Yes very witty. You won't be laughing when I slip your flattened bollocks into my wallet.

Frankie What, like you did four weeks ago?

Sweeney Was that on a certain night?

Frankie What night would that be?

Mugsy Oi!

Sweeney I forget, was it?

Frankie   Was it . . . no it couldn't have been –

Sweeney   I think it was . . .

Mugsy   Stop mentioning it, no one mentions the unmentionable!

Frankie   What? The unmentionable night you lost three grand to our beloved employer?

Mugsy   He should never've been in that hand. It was the outdraw of the century –

Sweeney   Tell us about it, Mugs.

Frankie   For a change.

Mugsy   It's Hold'em. I've got aces, right. It's my button, I raise before the flop, everyone passes, Stephen back-raises me, I think right, I'll slow-play from now on.

Frankie   Maestro!

Mugsy   What does it flop? Only queen, queen, ace, I've only flopped a house, I've only flopped the stone bonking unbeatable rock of Gibraltar Bank of England nuts.

Sweeney *and* **Frankie**   Yes!

Mugsy   The Turn, no help, I check.

Sweeney   Genius!

Mugsy   Last card, what comes? The only card I don't want to see, the only card that beats me.

Sweeney   A queen!

Frankie   That's when you should've passed.

Mugsy   I didn't know he'd made four queens!

Frankie   It was obvious, he bet a grand at you. Play the man not the cards. You fell in love with your hand.

Mugsy   Wouldn't you?

Frankie   You were unlucky.

Mugsy   Unlucky? Have you any idea what the odds are for him hitting a queen on the last card?

Frankie   Forty-three to one against.

Beat.

Mugsy   Er . . . yeah, exactly, forty-three to one against.

Sweeney   You were unlucky, Mugs, how many more times do you want to hear it?

Mugsy   Do you realise how many hours overtime I'm doing to pay off that debt? I haven't had a day off in three weeks, I'm working every Saturday night and I had to cancel my holiday, I was going to take my mum to Disneyland. I'd saved up specially.

Frankie   You still shouldn't have called on the end.

Mugsy   How can you pass aces?

Frankie   Sometimes you have to.

Mugsy   I know. I knew I'd lost but I still called. Why? Why did I call?

Frankie   Because you are a mug, Mugs.

Mugsy   It was so unfair.

Frankie   You expect justice at a poker table?

Mugsy   I'll win it back tonight, you'll see.

Sweeney   Win back three grand?

Mugsy   Where is he anyway, we're supposed to be discussing business.

Frankie   Probably ironing the baize. No crinkles on the baize –

Sweeney   No crinkles on the baize!

Mugsy   No crinkles on the baize!

Frankie   Fucking nutter.

Stephen *enters.*

Stephen   My children. The game is on. The Poker Room awaits.

Mugsy   At long last, it's like waiting for King Canute.

Pause.

Stephen   In what *possible* sense is it like waiting for King Canute?

Pause. **Mugsy** *is dumbfounded.*

Stephen   Downstairs, scum.

Frankie *and* **Sweeney** *exit.*

Mugsy   Right, Stephen, can we get down to business please?

Stephen   Just a moment.

Stephen *enters*

Restaurant.

Stephen   My son tells me you'd like to play with us tonight.

Ash   Yeah, if that's all right with you.

Stephen   I look forward to it.

Beat. They look at each other.

Your waiter will bring you down in a minute.

Stephen *exits into*

Kitchen.

Mugsy   Right, Stephen, business. Now, the key to this scheme is . . . flexibility. I see you as a man of vision and I see your role in this scheme as that of a silent partner, who can speak, but in a quiet advisory capacity . . . are you all right?

Stephen   Look, I have to tell you that I think my son is the last person in the world that anyone ought to go into business with.

Mugsy   You've got a very fair point.

Stephen   Mugsy, I don't want to disappoint you but –

Mugsy   It's all right, I've anticipated your concerns: you're worried I'll take Sweeney and Frankie with me, a reasonable anxiety for a proprietor; now I can offer you a job-share scheme whereby –

Stephen   No Mugs –

Mugsy   Is it because of the location?

Stephen   Of course not.

Mugsy   Is it because it's a toilet?

Stephen   I'm sorry?

Mugsy   Is it because the proposed property is at present a public convenience because once you've seen it you'll –

Stephen *bursts out laughing.*

Mugsy   What?

Stephen   I'm sorry, Mugs.

He laughs again.

Mugsy   Didn't Carl tell you?

Stephen   No, he most certainly did not. No, he edited that tiny piece of information right out of the scheme. I wonder why?

Stephen *laughs again.*

Mugsy   What exactly is the joke?

Stephen (*laughing*)   You want to open a restaurant in a toilet with my son – that'll do for me!

Mugsy   I thought you were a man of vision.

Stephen   Good evening, sir, your usual cubicle?

Mugsy   Why can't you just think about the idea, for one second without immediately –

Stephen   All right, I'm sorry, Mugs.

Mugsy   I'm not a mug, you know, I'm not in actual fact a mug.

Stephen   OK, I'm sorry.

Beat.

OK, seriously . . . don't you think it might be a problem with the ladies and gents having to dine separately?

He laughs again.

Mugsy   Will you fucking take me seriously! It can change, it's not going to be a toilet! What was this place before you bought it?

Stephen   A butcher's.

Mugsy   A butcher's, right, well, I don't see people coming in here saying 'I want to buy a pound of sausages'. People aren't going to come into my restaurant and have a crap on the dining-room floor. It's gonna change!

Stephen   Point taken.

Mugsy   You're treating me disrespectfully, Stephen, you can't push me about just cos you're in charge, I'm not your fucking son.

Stephen   What's that supposed to mean?

Mugsy   It's not difficult to run a restaurant I'll tell you that.

Stephen   Listen, Mugs, listen. I'm sorry for laughing, really. Look, we get on well you and I, we have good rapport, you're a much valued member of my staff.

Mugsy   Yeah, well.

Stephen   Yeah well what? It's true, you've been here since day one, the customers are very fond of you, you're indispensable.

Mugsy   You think I'm a good waiter?

Stephen   You're my top man, you're my head waiter.

Mugsy   What does that mean? You don't pay me more than anyone else, I'm working night and day for you, I'm working my balls off.

Stephen   You know why that is, Mugs. You're like family – better than family, we actually get on.

Mugsy   Exactly, so you don't want to lose me so you won't help me in my business, that's what's going on underneath. You can't see it cos it's buried so deep but I know you Stephen, I can read you, that's what I think.

Stephen   All right, that's what you think.

Mugsy   You want to hold me back.

Stephen   All right. You can choose to take this however you want but I think it's the truth. I think you're angry because you're paying off a poker debt in the only way you can which is by working overtime, by working your balls off –

Mugsy   No –

Stephen   Just let me finish please, and you find it humiliating – but there is no other way, I can't just scrub the debt.

Mugsy   You outdrew me.

Stephen   Yes I did, I'm sorry, it was bad luck. Nothing more, nothing less.

Mugsy   Yeah, but I'm the only one suffering for it.

Stephen   You lost, Mugsy, losing hurts.

Pause.

And this restaurant you want to open . . . it's not *real* Mugs
. . . opening a restaurant is a huge risk, nine out of ten don't
survive. You know nothing about this business; dealing with
suppliers, tax returns, employment law –

Mugsy   I could learn, you did.

Stephen   You could but it's hard.

Mugsy   I could do it.

Stephen   I'm not saying you couldn't.

Mugsy   You think it, you think I couldn't.

Stephen   I think . . . that you're good at the job that you
do. I also think that you don't, in your heart, really *want* to
open a restaurant. I think it scares you. And I think you're
disappointed with yourself that it scares you. Believe me,
Mugs, I do understand disappointment.

Pause.

Mugsy   That's what you think, is it?

Stephen   That's what I think.

Beat.

Mugsy   I've got to . . .

Stephen   OK?

Mugsy   Yeah, OK.

Stephen   I'm going downstairs. OK.

Mugsy   YES OK.

Stephen *turns at exit.*

Stephen   Mugsy . . . will you bring him down for me
please?

Mugsy   Yeah.

Stephen *exits.* **Mugsy** *sits alone in the kitchen. He takes his shirt off and puts on a bright Hawaiian shirt from his bag and also the new tie he was wearing earlier.*

Enter **Frankie**.

Frankie   So?

Mugsy   He's interested . . . he's definitely interested. He's having a think about it but he's interested.

Frankie   Great.

Beat.

You coming down?

Mugsy   Yeah. (*Pause. He turns to* **Frankie**.) *Am* I a mug?

Frankie (*gently*)   Course you're not.

He takes the pack of cards from the kitchen table.

Come on, we're starting.

Mugsy   Yeah.

Frankie *exits riffling the deck.* **Mugsy** *exits into*

Restaurant.

Mugsy   We're starting.

Ash   Right. Nice shirt.

Mugsy   Thanks . . . lucky poker shirt.

He leads **Ash** *out of the restaurant and through the kitchen.*

It's this way . . .

He stops at the exit.

You say you're in the investment business?

Ash (*off*)   Yeah.

Mugsy   Do you know the Mile End Road?

Act Three

Scene One

Basement.

Late night.

The atmosphere of this room should be noticeably different from the sleek environments of Acts One and Two. A battered fridge, **Stephen***'s desk with a computer on it and a framed photo of* **Carl***, aged five, filing cabinets, empty crates etc.*

The game is in progress. The players are seated at a table covered with a green baize cloth. **Ash** *at one o'clock,* **Carl** *at three,* **Sweeney** *five,* **Frankie** *seven,* **Mugsy** *nine and* **Stephen** *at eleven.* **Ash** *has just dealt. They are playing 'Omaha'. Each player has four cards in his hand. This is the first round of betting.*

Carl   Call. (*He puts in two pounds in chips.*)

Sweeney   Okey Dokey. (*Likewise.*)

Frankie   Call. (*Etc.*)

Mugsy   I call.

Stephen   Yup.

Ash   Raise ten.

Carl   No. (*He passes his cards into the middle.*)

Sweeney   Yep.

Frankie   Call.

Mugsy   Calling for the value.

Frankie   You tilty bastard!

Mugsy   I'm not on tilt.

Frankie   You're horizontal.

Mugsy Just for that I shall re-raise, the bet is Tony's pregnant sister.

Stephen What?

Mugsy Fifteen, mate!

Laughter.

Stephen (*referring to the tie*) I thought I told you to remove that monstrosity.

Mugsy Your dictatorship ended two hours ago. Poker law has been declared. The tie stays. Your bet, Stevie boy.

Stephen Don't call me that. Pass.

Mugsy *makes chicken noises.*

Mugsy Go on, Stevie boy, have a flutter for once in your life, you granite bastard!

Stephen It's poker, Mugsy, not the bloody lottery.

Mugsy Poker without gambling is like sex without orgasm.

Frankie What would you know? Last time Mugsy had an orgasm you know what came out . . . dust.

Mugsy Losing tonight are you by any chance, Francis?

Frankie Switch off.

Stephen Gentlemen, we have a guest.

Ash Fifteen, call.

Sweeney Yep.

Frankie Call. Flop 'em.

Ash *deals the flop, i.e. he turns over three 'communal' cards face up on the table.*

Ash Jack of spades, seven of spades, ten of diamonds.

Mugsy   Deemonds! (*A refrain he shouts whenever a diamond is dealt.*)

Sweeney   Fifty quid.

Frankie   Call.

Mugsy   Oh, my good friend, I'm afraid I'm going to have to raise your arse. There's your fifty and I raise one hundred pounds sterling.

Sweeney   Want a caller, Mugs?

Mugsy   Two preferably.

Frankie   Reckon your straight's gonna stand up?

Mugsy   More than your trips are, loser.

Ash   I raise . . . three hundred.

Laughter.

Sweeney   Pass.

Frankie   Pass. Bye bye, Mugsy.

Mugsy   Three hundred?

Frankie   Three hundred.

Mugsy   Three hundred?

Ash   Three hundred.

Sweeney   THREE HUNDRED.

Carl   Pass, Mugsy.

Frankie   What a poker face!

Mugsy   Shut up, I'm thinking.

Sweeney   We can see that, we can see your brain sweating, it's dribbling out your arse'ole, mate!

Mugsy   Shut up. Who raised before the flop?

All   You!

Laughter.

Mugsy   He must have the eight nine of spades. I can't call.

Stephen   Is that a pass, Mugs?

Mugsy   No.

Stephen   Come on, it's not chess.

Mugsy   Yeah, well, you obviously haven't read Herbert O. Yardley, 'Poker is chess with money'.

Stephen   Not the way you play it.

Mugsy   What day is it?

Sweeney   Oh, for fuck's sake, Sunday.

Stephen   Monday actually.

Mugsy   No, I meant what date.

Carl   The ninth.

Mugsy   Odd number, right . . . no, hold on . . . How much is in the pot?

Carl   About five hundred.

Frankie   Here Mugs, that's half a toilet!

Laughter.

Stephen   Actually, Frankie, it's one sixth of a toilet. You never were very good at maths –

Carl   Pass, Mugsy.

Sweeney   Come on, you mug, I'm growing a beard here.

Mugsy   Shut up, it's a big pot, PLEASE. Eight nine of spades. He's got eight nine of spades . . . I'd stake my reputation on it.

Ash   I'd prefer your money.

Pause.

Mugsy   Call.

Stephen   The bet is called.

Mugsy   He's bluffing.

Frankie   Bollocks.

Ash   OK?

Mugsy   Oh yes.

Ash *deals another card face up.*

Ash   Four of diamonds.

Mugsy   Deemonds!

Ash   Your bet.

Mugsy   One hundred and forty-six all in.

Ash   Call.

Mugsy   Shit.

Frankie   He's got eight nine of spades.

Mugsy   That's where you're wrong, the reason why I called is that I had a hunch he had eight nine of spades but I distrusted my hunch because I've had a cold recently.

Stephen   Come on, on their backs.

Mugsy *and* **Ash** *turn their cards over. Laughter.*

Mugsy   I don't believe it, I do not believe it! Eight nine of spades. (*To* **Ash**.) Don't turn a spade over, don't turn a spade over. No spade, no spade, DON'T TURN A FUCKING SPADE OVER! I can't look . . . Frankie, tell me what comes.

Mugsy *turns away.* **Ash** *turns a card over.*

Frankie   Ten of spades . . . tough luck, Mugs.

Mugsy   Fuck, fuck, fuck, fuck, fuck, fuck, fuck, fuck.

Frankie   Sorry, my mistake, ten of clubs, split pot.

Mugsy (*relieved*)   You cunt!

Laughter.

Frankie   Trick of the light, mate.

Stephen   Come on, split it up. Half each.

Mugsy   Jesus, my whole life just flashed before my eyes.

Frankie   Any good?

Mugsy   No, *you* were in it.

Stephen   Next case.

Mugsy (*to* **Ash**)   Sorry, mate, I lost my cool there for a second.

Laughter.

Ash   I think I've got a full house.

Laughter stops.

Stephen   Where?

Ash   There, it paired the board. Tens on Jacks.

Carl   He's right . . .

Ash   Sorry, mate.

Ash *rakes in the chips.*

Mugsy   Shit, I didn't see it. Fuck shit tit piss wank fuck bollocks.

Stephen   Bad luck, Mugs.

Mugsy   I've just done five hundred quid.

Frankie   The night is young.

Mugsy   Carl, you might have warned us – he's got the lot.

Ash   Beginner's luck.

Stephen   *Again.* Your deal, Carl.

Carl   Any requests?

Mugsy   Yeah, I'd like to win please.

Sweeney   He said requests not miracles.

Mugsy   You winning then, Sween?

Sweeney   No one's winning except *him*.

Carl   Five-card draw, jacks or better.

Scene Two

Later.

Sweeney (*singing to the tune of 'I Could've Danced All Night'*)   I haven't seen a card all night, I haven't seen a card all night. I haven't seen a card all night. Right, everyone, if I lose this lot I'm going.

Mugsy   Bye, mate. The Hospital for Poker Casualties is just along the road.

Stephen   Mugsy will show you the way.

Sweeney   One last shot.

Mugsy   And the game is Mugsy's Nightmare.

Stephen   Deal me out.

Mugsy (*to* **Ash**)   Stephen doesn't like Mugsy's Nightmare.

Stephen   I like playing poker not bloody roulette.

Frankie   You don't like playing poker, Stephen. You like winning.

Stephen   Thank you, Sigmund. Come on, Mugsy, choose a grown-up game.

Mugsy   It's Dealer's Choice. I'm the dealer I'll play what I want.

Sweeney   Just deal.

Mugsy *begins to deal two cards to each player.*

Mugsy   Out?

Stephen   Yes, OUT.

Mugsy   Ooo.

Sweeney   Will someone remind me of the rules of this ridiculous fucking game . . .

Mugsy   Five-card stud, hi-lo, two down, three up, whores, fours and one-eyed jacks wild, cards speak, eight or better for the low, the wheel goes, suicide king up you lose automatically.

Stephen   It's not poker, it's bloody bingo for brain surgeons. The game is like its inventor – a freak mutation.

Mugsy   So don't play, Lemon.

Stephen   I'm not playing, Toilet.

Mugsy   Ash?

Ash   Pass.

Stephen   Very wise.

Carl   Call two.

Mugsy   Good boy.

Sweeney   I call.

Frankie (*reluctant*)   Go on then.

Mugsy   No raise from the dealer.

He deals an up card to **Carl**, **Sweeney**, **Frankie** *and himself.*

Three of clubs, jack of clubs, two-eyed, six of deemonds and ten of deemonds. Double deemonds. Jack to speak.

Sweeney   Eight.

Frankie   Yeah.

Mugsy   One fat lezza going in.

Sweeney What?

Mugsy Eight.

Sweeney Well, say it.

Mugsy Ooo.

Carl Call eight.

Mugsy *deals another up card to* **Carl**, **Sweeney**, **Frankie** *and himself.*

Mugsy Nine of hearts busted low, five of clubs possible flush, seven of spades straightening, queen of hearts wild. Tens are on the potty. What is it?

Frankie Forty.

Mugsy Mid-life crisis, forty.

Carl Pass.

Sweeney Call.

Frankie Yep. How old are you, Stephen?

Stephen I can't remember.

Frankie Enjoying your mid-life crisis?

Stephen Yes, it began when you started working here.

Sweeney Can we play cards please?

Mugsy We can, dunno about you.

He deals an up card to **Sweeney**.

Eight of clubs, still possible . . .

And then **Frankie**.

King of hearts . . . bad luck, mate.

Frankie What d'you mean?

Mugsy Suicide king you lose automatically.

Frankie You what?

Mugsy   Bye bye.

Frankie   You never said.

All   Yes he did!

Beat.

Frankie   What a stupid poxy little game!

Stephen   You were warned.

Frankie   WHAT A FEEBLE FUCKING FARCE!

Sweeney   Could you please SHUT UP!

Mugsy   Shh, shh, everyone quiet for Sween, he's doing his bollocks, quiet.

Sweeney   Deal, Mugs.

Mugsy (*deals a final up card to himself*)   Four of hearts. Check.

Pause.

Sweeney (*to* **Frankie**)   You got that fifty?

Pause.

Frank . . . the fifty.

Frankie *gives* **Sweeney** *fifty pounds in cash.*

Sweeney   Let's see what you're made of, Mugsy. There's fifty plus forty . . . seven . . . that's ninety-seven all in.

Mugsy   Call.

Sweeney   What you got, Mugs?

Mugsy   Five tens.

Pause.

Sweeney   How the fuck can you have 'five tens', there's only four in the pack and I've got one of them.

Mugsy   I've got queen four in the box, my son, four wilds.

Mugsy *turns over his cards.*

Beat.

Sweeney   You win.

Mugsy   Yes! I wish you'd had more money, Sween, you'd have done your bollocks, roasted like a kipper, mate. It's my night, I told you, Mugsy's back, the Mug is back!

Frankie   You winning then?

Mugsy   No, but I'm on the way. What d'you have, Sween?

Sweeney   Flush.

Frankie   You can't call with that.

Sweeney   I just did.

Frankie   And you lost.

Sweeney   Yeah, all right.

Frankie   Just trying to help.

Sweeney   You winning?

Frankie   No but –

Sweeney   Well, then, stop being such an expert Mr Vegas.

Stephen   Lovers' tiff all over now, is it? Your deal, Frankie.

Sweeney *gets up.*

Sweeney   I'm out of here.

Frankie   Seven stud hi-lo.

Sweeney   Can I grab a beer, Stephen?

Stephen   Yup.

Sweeney *goes to the fridge but decides against taking a beer.* **Frankie** *starts to deal.*

Sweeney (*sings*)   I haven't seen a card all night, I haven't seen a card all night. I haven't seen a card all night, I –

Stephen   Sweeney.

Sweeney   Good evening?

Stephen   There's a game on . . .

Sweeney   Sorry, sorry.

Frankie (*to* **Mugsy**)   Your bet.

Sweeney   I haven't seen a card all night, I haven't seen a card all night, I haven't seen a card all night –

Stephen   Sweeney.

Sweeney   Your Highness?

Stephen   You know the house rules, Sweeney, if you're not in the game you're not in the room.

Sweeney   Sorry, I forgot.

Frankie   Mugs, you to bet.

Sweeney   I HAVEN'T SEEN A CARD ALL NIGHT, I HAVEN'T SEEN A CARD ALL NIGHT, I HAVEN'T SEEN A CARD ALL FUCKING NIGHT –

Stephen   If you're not in the game you're not in the room. House Rules.

Sweeney   What does it matter, Stephen, what the fuck does it matter?

Stephen   It matters, Sweeney, because rules are rules.

Sweeney   They're *your* rules, Stephen, no one else gives a flying fuck. 'No smoking' – have you ever heard anything so ridiculous for a poker school? No beers on the table unless they're on these poxy little beer mats. Oi . . . Ash, see this baize, this tatty bit of shit, he takes it home every Sunday night, religiously, and irons it, he fucking irons it, the c –

He is now close to tears.

See that computer, what does he keep on it? Accounts? Invoices? No, he keeps a record of all the games we've played, with lots of little coloured graphs and charts. He lives for his poker. He can tell you who won the game and with what hand on Easter Sunday six fucking years ago.

Stephen   Good night.

Sweeney   What is your problem?

Stephen   I don't think I have a problem. I just want to play a quiet game of cards on a Sunday night without you in the background sloshing around in a sea of self-pity. Call.

Ash   Call.

Carl   Call.

Sweeney   Come on, Frankie, let's go . . .

Frankie (*standing*)   I'd better get him home.

Stephen   It's your bet, Frankie.

Pause.

Frankie (*to* **Sweeney**)   You OK? I mean . . .

Pause.

Sweeney   No, you stay.

Frankie   Cheers . . . I'm doing my money here, mate, sorry.

Frankie *sits down.*

Sweeney   See you, guys.

Mugsy   See you, Sween.

Carl   Night, Sween.

Sweeney   Nice to meet you, Ash, I hope you win the fucking lot. I'll see you, Stephen.

Stephen   Sweeney, do you think you and Louise will manage to find somewhere with no entrance fees tomorrow?

You could try the Tate Gallery . . . is she fond of Giacometti?

Beat.

I'll see you first thing, Tuesday, lunch. Sweeney?

Sweeney (*in tears*)　Yeah.

Stephen　Here you are . . . fifty quid . . . overtime.

He holds up a fifty-pound note. **Sweeney** *hesitates but then approaches.*

Sweeney (*taking the note*)　Cheers.

Frankie　Sween . . .

Sweeney　No.

Sweeney *exits.*

Beat.

Ash　Your bet.

Frankie　Yep.

Carl　Eights or better?

Frankie　Yep.

Mugsy　The wheel goes?

Frankie　Uh-huh.

Stephen　With declarations?

Frankie　Cards speak. I raise.

Scene Three

Later.

Ash *and* **Stephen** *are offstage.*

Mugsy   So what exactly did you say to Stephen about the restaurant, Carl?

Carl   I'm sorry, Mugs, I tried, he just wasn't interested.

Ash*'s mobile phone starts to ring.*

Frankie   Aye aye.

Frankie *removes the phone from* **Ash***'s coat pocket. The phone continues to ring.*

Carl   Don't, Frankie.

Frankie   What? Might be important.

Carl   It's not your phone.

Frankie   All right, don't get your Y-fronts knotted, Carl.

Mugsy   Go on, answer it.

Carl   It's not your phone.

Mugsy   Maybe something's happened, might be urgent.

Frankie   Yeah and he gets called away with our money . . .

Frankie *gives the phone back to* **Carl** *as* **Stephen** *enters carrying a bottle of whisky.*

Stephen   Did he have that thing in the restaurant?

Mugsy   Yeah.

The phone stops ringing.

Stephen   Well I hope it didn't go off in there, it specifically says on the menu, 'No Mobile Phones'.

Frankie   What, might've disturbed the other customer?

Stephen   Where's he gone?

Carl   Cigarette, outside.

Mugsy (*Bogart*)   Can't play poker if you ain't a smoker.

Frankie   You don't smoke.

Beat.

Mugsy   Yeah . . . I know . . . but if I did.

Frankie   Do you smoke, Carlton?

Carl   Me? No.

Frankie   I wonder why.

Stephen   Could it be because it kills you? Be my guest, Frankie . . . outside. Actually, I've always thought it's a rather interesting tell . . . smoking. Who wants to live, who wants to die?

Mugsy   He's got a point.

Frankie   Judas.

Mugsy   Yeah, well, I'm pissed off with you chucking your fag-ends in my saddle-bag.

Frankie (*to* **Stephen**)   Hard to believe you were a sixty-a-day man.

Stephen   Forty. Your 'teacher' friend is rather good, Carl . . .

Carl   He's just being lucky, that's all.

Frankie (*riffling his chips*)   I'll sort him out.

Stephen   Oooh, big man. How long did he teach you for?

Carl   Two years.

Stephen   Funny I never met him . . .

Carl   Probably because you never came to visit.

Stephen   Yes I did.

Carl   Twice, in five years.

He goes to the fridge.

Beer anyone? Frankie?

Frankie   Yeah, cheers.

Stephen   What did you say he taught you?

Carl   I didn't.

Stephen   So what did he teach you?

Carl   General Studies. Mugs?

Mugsy   Is there a Tango in there?

Carl   Yeah, your flat one from last week.

Mugsy   Yeah, give it here. I won last week, must be a lucky can.

Carl *gives* **Mugsy** *the can.*

Mugsy   I thought it was Economics?

Carl   As part of General Studies.

Stephen   Curiouser and curiouser.

Mugsy   Think Sween's OK?

Frankie   Yeah, he was a bit pissed that's all.

Stephen   Probably not used to such fine claret.

Frankie   Here you are . . . Fagin.

He throws eighty pounds in chips to **Stephen**.

Stephen   Thank you . . . Dodger. Actually, you can have a discount for prompt payment.

He throws him a five-pound chip.

Frankie   Isn't staff discount ten per cent?

Stephen   That's if you're still on the staff.

Frankie   I might not be.

Ash *enters.*

Mugsy   Oi, mate, your mobile went off. It's OK though, we took a message, 'Give us the money or the kid gets it.'

Pause. **Ash** *looks worried.*

Carl   We let it ring.

Ash *sits down.*

Ash   Right. Hold 'em.

He begins to deal two down cards to each player.

Stephen   Ah, a man after my own heart.

Mugsy   Oi, Frankie, I forgot, what was she like?

Frankie   Who?

Mugsy   The bird last night.

Frankie   Never you mind.

Carl   Call.

Stephen   I fail to understand what these women see in you.

Frankie   Bit of rough, innit. Yep.

Mugsy   Rough deemond. I'm in.

Frankie   You should've seen him last night, he was well on the sniff.

Stephen   I can assure you I was not 'on the sniff'. She looked like Miss Albania 1975. Call.

Ash   No raise. The flop.

Ash *turns over three up cards.*

Frankie   Stevie boy doesn't like women Ash, prefers to surround himself with virile younger men. All stems from this high-stakes poker game he got involved in, lost half his income to a woman, game called . . . Divorce. You ever played that?

Ash   Yeah, but I won.

Frankie   Resulto, what d'you win?

Ash   My freedom. The flop is ace of clubs, four of clubs, seven of diamonds.

Mugsy   Deemonds!

Carl   Check.

Frankie   So ever since then he's become a bit of a . . .

Stephen   Oh, Frankie, and you were doing so well. The word you're groping for is –

Frankie   I know the word, 'misogynist'.

Stephen   That's the one.

Ash   Your bet.

Frankie   Check.

Stephen   And how are you spelling 'misogynist'?

Beat.

No, OK, we'll come back to you.

Frankie   I'm spelling it with an F for fuck –

Stephen   Too late, Frankie, the moment's gone.

Ash   Your bet.

Mugsy   Me? Check.

Stephen   Check.

Ash (*dealing the next card*)   Eight of diamonds.

Mugsy   Deemonds!

Frankie   WILL YOU FUCKING SHUT UP ABOUT YOUR FUCKING DEEMONDS!

Pause.

Carl *knocks indicating check,* **Frankie** *knocks,* **Mugsy** *knocks,* **Stephen** *knocks,* **Ash** *knocks and then deals the final card.*

Ash   Ace of spades.

Carl *knocks*, **Frankie** *knocks*, **Mugsy** *knocks*.

Stephen Ten.

Ash Raise, thirty.

Carl Pass.

Frankie Pass.

Mugsy Pass, the discipline of the man.

Stephen Pass, I can't call.

Mugsy Granite.

Stephen No, real discipline, Mugs. Look, (*He turns over his cards.*) kings in the box, aces on the board – I can't call. What d'you have?

Ash *shows his cards*.

Stephen He bluffed me! Carl, will you get this man out of here, please.

Mugsy House rules, mate, no bluffing the management.

Ash I'll bear it in mind.

Stephen Carl, your deal.

Carl Five-card draw, red threes and black twos wild.

Mugsy Yes!

Stephen Oh, for God's sakes, Carl let's not play silly games.

Carl It's Dealer's Choice!

Stephen You can't play draw with wild cards, it's a classic game you can't 'customise' it.

Carl Fine, we'll play Hold'em all night.

Stephen Don't be pathetic.

Frankie If you're gonna play stupid kids' games I might as well go and play 'rummy' with my nan.

Stephen   He's absolutely right.

Carl   It's Dealer's Choice.

Mugsy   'Cept when Stephen and Frankie don't like it.

Frankie   I'm going after the next hand.

Stephen   Now look what you've done.

Carl   I haven't done anything.

Stephen   Look, we've played silly buggers all night, can we please play some serious poker with no wild cards. I'm going for a piss. Discuss.

Stephen *exits.*

Mugsy   Frankie, don't go.

Frankie   There's no skill involved with wild cards, it's all luck.

Mugsy   And that's why you're going?

Frankie   Yeah.

Mugsy   No other reason you can think of? No? Cos it's just occurred to me that there might be another reason like for example the fact that for the first time in living memory you're actually losing.

Frankie   What and you're winning?

Mugsy   No, no I'm not, but at least I'm staying to the end, at least I'm a good loser.

Frankie   THAT'S WHY YOU'RE A LOSER. YOU MUG.

Pause.

Ash   Go on, Carl, deal a round of Hold'em while your dad's gone.

Carl   OK, Hold'em.

Carl *deals two down cards to each player.*

Mugsy   So what exactly did you say to him, Carl? Cos he didn't seem too keen, you were supposed to soften him up.

Carl   I did my best, Mugs, I'm sorry.

Frankie   Ten to play.

Mugsy   Pass.

Ash   Call.

Carl   Not for me. The flop . . .

He deals three cards up.

Three of hearts, king of clubs, jack of hearts.

Frankie   Fifty.

Ash   Call.

Carl *deals another card up.*

Carl   Ten of diamonds.

Beat.

Mugsy   Deemonds.

Frankie *looks at him.*

Frankie   Hundred.

Ash   Call.

Carl *deals the final up card.*

Carl   Nine of spades.

Beat.

Frankie   Four hundred and twenty-five, all in.

Ash   Call.

Pause.

I'm seeing you.

Pause.

Frankie   Nothing . . .

Ash   Pair of threes.

Ash *rakes in the chips.*

Frankie   How can you call with a pair of threes?

Ash   Fancied it.

Frankie   D'you see that, Mugs? He called four hundred with a pair of threes?

Mugsy   'Play the man not the cards.'

Beat.

Frankie   How d'you know?

Ash   Know what?

Frankie   That I was bluffing.

Ash   I guessed.

Frankie   You guessed for more than six hundred quid?

Ash   Guess so.

Frankie   Bollocks.

Carl   Frankie.

Frankie   Fuck off. How d'you know?

Beat.

Ash   You've got a tell.

Frankie   Me? What tell?

Ash   That'd be telling.

Frankie   Yeah, I ain't got a tell, you just tilted in like a mug.

Beat.

Ash   D'you really want to know what your tell is?

Frankie Yeah.

Ash Sure?

Frankie Yes.

Beat.

Ash When you bluff you look scared.

Silence.

Who's deal?

Carl Frankie's . . .

Mugsy How much you up?

Ash I dunno, couple of grand.

Mugsy Nice. I expect you'll be doing a bit of investing with that quite soon?

Ash Yeah.

Mugsy Cos, you know I was telling you about this property in Mile End –

Frankie It's not a property it's a toilet.

Ash It's a toilet?

Mugsy It's an extremely large public convenience smack bang in the middle of the Mile End Road. It's thirties. Art deco.

Frankie Is it fuck.

Mugsy It would make a fantastic restaurant.

Frankie Bollocks.

Ash There are precedents.

Mugsy Are there?

Ash Sure.

Frankie Who the fuck are you?

Mugsy FRANKIE, I AM IN A BUSINESS MEETING! (*To* **Ash**.) What presidents?

Ash (*to* **Carl**) You know my snooker club, that used to be a toilet.

Carl Still is.

Mugsy I can have mine for a grand.

Ash Cheap.

Mugsy Yeah. D'you reckon it could work, something like this but with a Frenchy/Italianey flavour in the Mile End neighbourhood?

Ash Yeah, I bet they're gagging for some of that in the Mile End neighbourhood.

Frankie *gets up from the table and puts on his coat.* **Stephen** *enters.*

Mugsy Would you come and have a look next week?

Ash Yeah, love to.

Mugsy Yeah, brilliant, I'll get your number off Carl. Thanks, thank you. I'll ring you tomorrow.

Ash Always here.

Stephen I'm frightfully sorry, have I interrupted a board meeting?

Mugsy Never you mind.

Stephen Whose deal? Frankie? Frankie?

Pause. **Stephen** *looks at him, concerned.*

Frankie I'm out.

Frankie *exits.*

Mugsy Right, my deal. Let's play . . . any requests?

Stephen Hold'em.

Mugsy Ash?

Ash Omaha.

Mugsy Let's play . . . a game for men of vision . . .
Omaha.

Scene Four

Later.

Ash Call.

Mugsy (*shows his cards*) Trip sixes . . . ?

Ash Sorry, mate, I've got a straight.

Mugsy Yeah, I thought you might. Last card?

Ash Yuh.

Ash *rakes in the chips.* **Mugsy** *is devastated.*

Stephen Is that it, Mugs?

Mugsy Yep, no more.

Carl Bad luck, Mugs.

Mugsy I've just been so unlucky.

Beat.

I've done a grand . . . I've done a fucking grand. Fuck.

Stephen Mugs, go home, get some sleep.

Mugsy Yeah. Listen, can I have a word with you,
Stephen, it's just . . . I . . . I've only got four hundred in cash
. . . I'm not sure whether my cheque . . .

Ash I'm going for a smoke.

Mugsy Sorry to break up the game.

Ash That's all right. Carl.

Carl *stands*. **Ash** *exits*.

Mugsy   Sorry, Carl, it's just –

Carl   It's all right Mugs.

Carl *exits*. **Stephen** *watches him go*.

Mugsy   I'm sorry, I thought I was going to win so I'd be able to –

Stephen   It's all right, Mugsy.

Mugsy   I mean, can you dock it off my wages?

Stephen   Yuh, it's fine.

Mugsy   I'll do more overtime so I can –

Stephen   I just said it's fine. We'll sort it out tomorrow.

Beat.

Mugsy, this restaurant of yours, how much did you and Carl want to borrow to secure the premises?

Mugsy   A grand.

Beat.

Stephen   *One* thousand pounds. You're sure?

Mugsy   Course I'm sure. I do know how it sounds . . . a toilet in Mile End but it could've worked if you'd have . . .

Stephen   You don't give up, do you? It's not easy, you know. Running a restaurant.

Mugsy   No I know, I mean I don't know but –

Stephen   Working with people like Sweeney and Frankie – Frankie, how would you deal with that?

Mugsy   I wouldn't employ Frankie.

Stephen   And now you're going to get this Ash 'character' to invest in you?

Mugsy   He did say he'd come and have a look.

Stephen   So *he's* your man?

Mugsy   No, *you* were my first choice. You still are.

Stephen   You should be careful, you know. *I'm* the businessman, I'm the restaurateur, I could take your idea, buy the premises tomorrow and cut you out like that.

Mugsy   Yeah but you wouldn't. I trust you.

Stephen   We're on the same level of circles?

Mugsy   Words to that effect.

Enter **Carl** *and* **Ash**.

Carl   OK?

Stephen   Yes, come in, join the party, there must be so much to talk about!

Carl   Yes. Listen, Mugsy . . . I've won . . . I can pay you, why don't I pay you the five hundred I owe you? Here . . . (*He stacks five hundred pounds in chips.*) thanks for the loan.

Mugsy   Are you sure?

Carl   Of course I'm sure, I owe it to you.

Mugsy   Thanks, Carl!

Carl   No problem.

Stephen   Anyone else?

Carl   Yeah, I was just about to. A hundred pounds as promised. Thanks, Dad.

He gives **Stephen** *one hundred pounds in chips.*

Stephen   The Prodigal Son.

Mugsy   Whose deal?

Stephen   What?

Mugsy   Whose deal?!

Stephen   It's over, Mugs, the game is over.

Mugsy   Bollocks it is, I've got five hundred quid here!

Stephen   Are you fucking mad?

Mugsy   No, are you scared, Stephen? Scared my luck's going to change? Come on, half an hour, come on . . . Carl?

Carl   I don't mind.

Mugsy   Ash?

Ash   Yeah, if you want.

Stephen   I'm not playing.

Mugsy   Why not?

Carl   Come on, Dad –

Stephen (*to* **Mugsy**)   Why can't you call it a night?

Mugsy   Because I want to win my money back.

Stephen   That's not the reason, it's you, you can't stop, it's no fun for you unless you lose.

Mugsy   I don't want to lose! Deal, Carl!

Stephen   Yes you do, you're addicted to it. You can't stop punishing yourself.

Mugsy   *Deal*, Carl.

Stephen   Mugsy, I'm trying to protect you.

Mugsy   From what?

Stephen   What do you think?

Mugsy   I don't know, what?

Stephen   From yourself!

Mugsy   I don't need protecting from myself, I'm my own best friend. I'm on my side.

Stephen   *I'm* on your side.

Mugsy   Bollocks, you're on your side, he's on his side, Carl's on his side, I'm on my side. Just deal! Someone! Please!

Carl   Hold'em.

Stephen   You're mad!

Mugsy   Yeah yeah.

Carl   Hold'em, just for you, Dad.

Carl *deals two down cards to each player.*

Stephen   I'm out.

Mugsy   Half an hour, half an hour.

Stephen   Look at him, he's like a junkie with a new fix. Correction, he *is* a junkie with a new fix!

Mugsy   Ten. Stephen.

Stephen   No!

Mugsy   Your bet.

Stephen   No!

Mugsy   Your bet.

Stephen   No!

Mugsy   Your bet.

Stephen   No!

Mugsy   Bet or pass. Bet or pass, Stephen!

Beat.

Stephen   Call.

Mugsy   Good man!

Ash   Call.

Mugsy   Good man!

Carl   Game on.

Mugsy   Coming to get you, boys, you know what the good book says, 'early leaders, morning bleeders'. Flop 'em.

Carl *deals the flop.*

Mugsy   Deemonds!

Stephen   They're back.

Mugsy   Check.

Stephen   Forty.

Ash   Pass.

Carl   No.

Mugsy   Gotcha! I call the forty and raise a hundred and twenty.

Stephen   Got a good hand, Mugsy?

Mugsy   Cashews and almonds, mate, otherwise known as 'the nuts'.

Stephen   I call.

Mugsy   Thus he enters the poker graveyard.

Carl   Two of clubs.

Beat. **Mugsy** *looks worried.*

Stephen   Coffin for Mr Mugsy?

Mugsy   Check.

Stephen   Not so nutty now, eh? How much have you got left?

Mugsy   Three hundred and thirty.

Stephen   That's the bet.

Mugsy   I don't believe it. I've got top trips on the flop and then a fucking flush comes.

Stephen   Tell you what, stick your tie in as well and we'll call it an even three fifty.

Mugsy   The tie is worth *thirty*.

Stephen   All right, three sixty. Come on, Mugs, stick your money in, lose the pot and bugger off home.

Mugsy (*taking off his tie*)   Fuck it, call! Come on, on their backs, Stephen, there you go trip queens, what have you got?

Stephen   No, I'll let you suffer.

Mugsy   Don't fuck about, Stephen, on their backs!

Stephen   No, Mugsy, you need to learn your lesson.

Carl   Dad –

Stephen   *Deal*, Carl.

Mugsy   No, backs!

Carl   Dad, house rules.

Stephen   Just *deal*.

Mugsy   Backs!

Stephen   Deal!

Mugsy   Tell me what you've got.

Stephen   There's a card to come.

Carl   He must have the flush.

Mugsy   I know he must.

Stephen   *Deal*, Carl.

Mugsy   All right, pair the board, pair the fucking board!

Mugsy *starts to pray.* **Carl** *deals the final up card.*

Carl   Six of hearts.

Mugsy   NOOOOHH!!

He falls to the floor.

Stephen (*throwing his cards in*)   You win, Mugs.

Mugsy YES! Yes! The Mug is back. It's a miracle! What did you have, Stephen?

Stephen Trip fours.

Mugsy Trip fours, bottom trips and you raised? You're losing it, mate, you're cracking up!

He rakes in the chips.

It's what I always say Ash, this game is about stamina. It's about never say die even when you're dead. I have risen from the ashes like the proverbial dodo. I am resurrected. It took the Lord three days, the Mug one hand! Trip fours and he calls a back-raise on that flop . . . you've lost it, mate!

Stephen Yes all right, Mugs.

Mugsy You are on tilt mate and I am rolling, The Mug Is On A Roll! Whose deal?

Carl Yours.

Mugsy Right. I'm going for a dump. I may be gone some time. But when I return I shall take you boys so deeply to the cleaners you will never have to wash again!

Mugsy *exits and almost immediately re-enters, sniffing intently.*

Stephen What's wrong?

Mugsy Sorry, I thought I could smell something . . .

Stephen What?

Mugsy Fear, mate, *fear*!

Mugsy *exits.*

Ash Round of Omaha while we're waiting? Carl.

Carl *begins to deal four cards down to each player.*

Stephen How much are you up?

Ash About three grand.

Stephen *Three?* The magic number. Is that enough?

Ash   More is always welcome.

They look at their cards. **Ash**'s *mobile starts to ring.*

Stephen   Yours, I believe?

Ash *gets up.*

Stephen   Don't mind us.

Ash *exits with the phone.*

Stephen   Nice chap, don't you think? Shall we make him a regular?

Carl   I know what you did. That last pot Mugsy just 'won' . . . you lost on purpose. You never had trip fours.

Stephen   Yes I did.

Carl   I *passed* trip fours. You lost on purpose, *why*?

Stephen   Because . . .

Carl   Because you pitied Mugsy? So it's not even an honest game . . .

Stephen   Don't you talk to me about *honesty*, Carl.

Carl   You think you've done him a favour?

Stephen   Yes, I've made him happy.

Carl   And what if he found out?

Stephen (*urgently*)   Well, he's not going to find out, *is he*?

Carl   You just *gave* him a grand.

Stephen   He *needs* it.

Carl   And this evening you made me feel like shit about a hundred quid.

Stephen   I've got a feeling we're talking about a little bit more than a hundred pounds, Carl . . .

Carl   But you did give me shit about a hundred quid.

Stephen *And?*

Carl How am I supposed to feel?

Stephen You tell me.

Carl I feel . . . why *him*? What have you got against me?

Stephen (*passionately*) Carl . . . *no* . . . it's not like that. Do you think I . . . don't you *see*? Mugsy can't *survive* . . . you're different, don't you see? You're a talented boy. It's totally different . . . you're my *son*.

Ash *enters.*

Ash I've got to go. *Now.* It's urgent.

Stephen Someone not done their homework?

Pause.

Ash I've got to cash in.

Stephen But we're in the middle of a hand.

Ash Look, I've got a problem here . . . your son –

Stephen Scared? Come on . . . be a sport.

Carl *Please*, Ash.

Beat.

Ash OK, last hand. You want to play no limit?

Stephen Yeah, if you like.

Ash Great.

Stephen What do you think of Marx's theory of the inevitable decline of capitalism?

Ash Unlikely. Look at us.

Carl Omaha.

Stephen How much did you say you were up?

Ash About three grand.

Stephen   Is three enough, Carl?

Carl   Dad, let me explain, the original outlay –

Stephen   Ten.

Carl   The original –

Stephen   TEN. Sir?

Ash   Call ten.

Carl   Pass.

He deals the flop.

King . . . jack . . . jack . . .

Stephen   Check.

Ash   Fifty.

Stephen   Call.

Carl *deals the next up card.*

Carl   Seven of clubs.

Stephen   Check.

Ash   Hundred.

Stephen (*to* **Carl**)   Do you think I'm stupid?

Carl   No.

Stephen   Call.

Carl *deals the final up card.*

Carl   Ace of hearts.

Stephen   Check. How much do you owe him?

Carl   What are you talking about?

Stephen   Give me at least a modicum of respect.

Carl   I don't owe anything.

Stephen   DON'T LIE TO ME, CARL.

Beat.

Are you going to make a bet?

Ash   Yeah, I'll make a bet. Five hundred.

Stephen   Raise. There's your five and I raise one thousand and twenty-six, all in.

Beat.

Professor?

Beat.

One thousand and twenty-six.

Beat.

Yes?

Ash   I'm thinking.

Stephen   Think away.

Beat.

Ash   Call. House of jacks.

Stephen   House of kings.

Pause.

Oh dear.

He rakes in the chips.

Goodbye, Mr Chips.

Enter **Mugsy**.

Mugsy   Deal me in!

Stephen   Sorry, Mugs, game's over.

Mugsy   Yeah but . . .

Stephen   Game's over, everybody's far too tired.

Mugsy *makes chicken noises.*

Stephen   Yeah yeah.

Mugsy   Stephen?

Stephen   Mugsy.

Pause. **Mugsy** *understands 'something's happened'.*

Mugsy   All right, if you can't take the punishment I will spare you but next time, no mercy.

Carl   You poker genius.

Stephen   Are you up now, Mugsy?

Mugsy   Hold on, let me count . . . I most certainly am . . . I am winning, I am winning . . . I am winning . . . seven quid! I feel like I've won seven million though. You've got to stick at this game, if you don't suffer you don't improve. Am I right, Ash? Ash?

Stephen   You're absolutely right and with your winnings you can even get yourself a cab home.

Mugsy   I'm going home in a limo mate, I'm flying home in a Lear jet. Only joking, I'm on my bike. How much you up, Stephen?

Stephen   Hard to say. I think I'm winning though.

Mugsy   See, he never loses. Carl?

Carl   I don't know.

Mugsy   Ash? Oi, Ashy boy? How much you up?

Pause.

Stephen   Mr Ash has just lost a very big pot.

Mugsy   Oh right, sorry, mate. You're still well up though aren't you? What a result! Do you realise I shall not have to suffer another week of abuse in the kitchen. I shall laud it over Frankie and Sweeney as befits a *winner*.

Carl   Of seven quid.

Mugsy   It's not about amounts, young Carl, it's about winners and losers and we are winners! Oh, Ashy boy, I'll give you a ring tomorrow about the restaurant. I just had a thought actually, on the bog, if we gave it an oriental feel we could call it –

Ash   Why don't you fuck off.

Pause.

Stephen   Mugsy, go *home*.

Mugsy   Right, night, everyone. (*He checks his watch.*) Morning rather.

Carl   Mugsy . . . that pot you just won . . .

Beat.

Mugsy   What?

Carl *looks at* **Stephen**.

Carl   Here's your winnings.

He hands **Mugsy** *seven pounds.*

Mugsy   Oh yeah, cheers.

Stephen   Well played, Mugsy.

Mugsy   Class always tells, Stephen, in the end. See you!

Mugsy *exits.*

Stephen   Go and make some coffee, Carl.

Carl   Dad, I'm sorry –

Ash   Do as he says.

Stephen   Black, no sugar.

Carl *exits.*

Beat.

Ash   You played the hand well.

Stephen   Thank you. Got any kids?

Ash   No.

Stephen   Do you want a drink?

Ash   I don't.

Stephen   Why not?

Ash   I used to.

Beat.

Stephen   So . . .

Ash   He owes me four grand.

Stephen   Oh, four was it. How?

Ash   Gambling debt.

Stephen   When?

Ash   All this year, mainly poker but I lent him for roulette, blackjack, you name it.

Stephen   Where did you meet?

Ash   Casino.

Stephen   Why?

Ash   Why what?

Stephen   Why lend him?

Ash   Liked him, saw myself, that bollocks.

Stephen   And he liked you . . .

Ash   Look, I'm not here to talk about your son, he means nothing to me now. He was value.

Stephen   Fellow compulsive gambler?

Ash   I'm not a compulsive gambler, I do it for a living.

Stephen   Sounds compulsive to me.

Ash   No, you're wrong. *You're* the compulsive.

Stephen   What?!

Ash   Yeah, anyway who cares? The point is I'm owed four grand and I'd very much appreciate it now.

Stephen   I'm sure you would.

Ash   Come on, you have to pay it.

Stephen   What on earth for? My son owes it to you, get it off him.

Ash   He hasn't got it. Come on, it's a debt, I owe this money.

Stephen   What do you mean I'm a compulsive gambler?

Ash   You're doing it now.

Beat.

You're like him, you need the action.

Stephen   And you don't?

Ash   I need the money.

Stephen   You do this for a living, you must have money.

Ash   I live in a fucking bedsit.

Stephen (*mock sympathy*)   Ahh.

Ash *approaches.*

Ash   Give me the money.

Stephen   Don't you come near me.

Ash (*close*)   Scared? Excited? Turned on?

Beat.

Ash *lifts his arm as if to strike* **Stephen**. **Stephen** *flinches.*

Ash   Tell you what, I'll toss you for it.

Stephen   What?!

Ash   I'll toss you for it, go on, the whole lot, four grand, I'll toss you for it.

Stephen   You're out of your mind.

Ash   Go on. You know you want to.

Stephen   I most certainly do not.

Ash (*seductively*)   I think you do. You could clear the debt in one second. Be a hero. Live a little . . . for *once* in your fucking life. Go on.

Stephen   No.

Ash   Call.

Stephen   No.

Ash   Come on, *call* . . .

Stephen   No.

Ash   Call.

Stephen   No.

Ash   Call.

Stephen   NO.

Ash   CALL.

Stephen   NO.

Ash   CALL.

Stephen   NO.

Ash   CALL.

Stephen   NO.

Ash   CALL.

Stephen   NO.

Ash   CALL.

Stephen   NO.

Ash   CALL, YOU YELLOW CUNT!

Stephen   HEADS!

Ash *flips the coin, catches it and holds it in his clenched fist. Both men stare at the fist. Five seconds. Without revealing the coin* **Ash** *puts it back in his pocket.*

Ash   Four grand on the toss of a coin?

Pause.

Stephen   Take it.

Ash *goes to the chip box and counts the cash quickly.* **Stephen** *watches him, deflated.*

Stephen   How did you know?

Ash   It's my job.

He holds up a bundle of cash to **Stephen**.

Four grand, want to count?

Stephen   No . . . I trust you.

Ash   Right. I'm off then, thanks for the game.

Stephen   Where are you going?

Ash   Another game.

Stephen   It's the morning.

Ash   Yeah, must dash.

Stephen   This other game, is that where you owe the money?

Ash   Yeah.

Stephen   Are you the mug?

Pause.

Ash   I don't know.

Pause.

Hey . . . I'm sorry. About Carl.

Stephen   Thank you.

Ash   Bit like aces, kids, I suppose. You fall in love with them, you can't pass . . .

Stephen   Yuh . . . sometimes you have to.

Carl *enters.* **Ash** *looks at him.* **Ash** *exits.* **Carl** *puts the coffee on the table.*

Carl   Coffee.

Stephen   Thank you. See, you could still make a good waiter.

Carl   Ha Ha. If you're going to give me a bollocking will you just do it please . . .

Stephen   Is that what this is to you? A bollocking. I'm not your headmaster.

Silence.

He looks into the chip box.

Look, all the money's gone, we've been robbed. Where can it be?

Carl   Well, presumably you gave it to Ash.

Beat.

Stephen   Yuh. Did I have any choice?

Carl   Yes, you could've said no. You didn't have to protect me. You don't have to always be there for me.

Stephen   I'm your father.

Carl   So?

Stephen   So . . . everything.

Beat.

Carl   Why won't you let me fail?

Stephen   I am, you're doing great.

Carl   There's nothing wrong with failure as long as it's on your own terms.

Stephen   There's your mother!

Carl   Why are you like this?

Stephen   I'm not *like* anything. This is what I *am*.

Pause.

Carl, I don't want you to end up like . . . Ash. Do you think he's happy?

Carl   I'm doing OK.

Stephen   You're doing nothing.

Carl   I'm doing fine.

Stephen   You're doing fuck all. You're a waste of life, Carl. Don't take this personally, I'm just making observations.

Beat.

You have lied to me for a whole year.

Carl   I'm sorry.

Stephen   You've been coming in here every Sunday night 'Hi, Dad' 'Bye, Dad' and then you've gone straight off to a casino to gamble thousands of pounds with another man.

Carl   And you're *jealous*.

Pause.

Stephen   God, don't you just *love* Mugsy? I mean, he's *straight*. For all his bull-headed stupidity, for all his relentless inability to recognise his own inadequacy, that man is psychotically *alive*.

Carl   Fuck you! What you mean is he's *controllable*. Fuck you!

Stephen   The worm has turned . . .

Carl   Look at you with your pissy little poker game . . . which gives you the illusion of power. I've played with *real* men for *real* money. Ash lost every penny he ever had in *one night*.

Stephen   The object of the game is to win.

Pause.

Carl (*quietly*)   You don't understand.

Stephen   Yes I do.

Carl *goes to exit and then turns.*

Pause.

Carl   Same time next week?

Stephen *looks at him. Long silence.*

Carl   Night.

Carl *exits.*

Pause.

Stephen *sits at his desk and turns on the computer. The screen flashes into life revealing graphs and charts. He stares at the screen.*

Slow fade.

After Miss Julie

A version of Strindberg's *Miss Julie*

For Andrew

After Miss Julie was first broadcast on BBC Television on 4 November 1995, with the following cast:

Miss Julie	Geraldine Somerville
John	Phil Daniels
Christine	Kathy Burke
Music	Colin Good
Costume	Jill Taylor
Make Up	Jean Speak
Sound	John Relph
Camera	Peter Woodley
Editor	Judith Robson
Lighting	Chris Townsend
Designer	Sarah Greenwood
Producer	Fiona Finlay
Director	Patrick Marber

The stage premiere was at the Donmar Warehouse, London on 20 November 2003 with the following cast:

Miss Julie	Kelly Reilly
John	Richard Coyle
Christine	Helen Baxendale
Director	Michael Grandage
Designer	Bunny Christie
Lighting	Neil Austin
Sound	Matt McKenzie for Autograph

Characters

Miss Julie, *aged twenty-five*
John, *her father's chauffeur / valet, thirty*
Christine, *a cook, thirty-five*

Scene

The kitchen of a large country house outside London.

Time

26 July 1945. Night and the morning after.

The British Labour Party won their famous 'landslide' election victory on this night.

The kitchen is a large room on basement level. It's a little gone to seed, neglected. A door leads out to an unseen exterior courtyard and beyond where a dance is in progress. Other doors lead off to the servants' living quarters. In the centre of the room is a large wooden table, chairs at either end, benches at the sides. On the table a pair of black brogues, polish and brushes. Elsewhere a bell and phone system for communication with other areas of the house.

Big band dance music from outside continuing throughout the first sequence of the play.

Christine *is alone at a large range, frying kidneys. She is wearing a summer dress with a cooking apron over it.*

After a while, **John** *enters. He wears a chauffeur's uniform. He carries a newspaper, the London edition of 'The Evening News'. He puts his car keys in a small cupboard by the door. He goes to the sink and washes his face and hands.*

John Sorry.

Christine It's gone midnight.

John I'm sorry.

Christine I've eaten.

John I had to drive his Lordship to London for the celebrations; big do at Central Hall. Police waved us straight through. You should've seen the crowds.

Christine I heard you park half an hour ago.

John Well, I stopped off at the barn – just to show my face. But then Miss Julie flounces up and says 'Partner me'. I couldn't say no.

He sits at the table.

She's off her head, dancing with everyone and anyone, making a right exhibition of herself. She's barking mad, that one.

Christine Don't be rotten. She's lovesick, poor thing.

John (*sighs*)   'The Reluctant Officer'.

Beat.

D'you reckon it's odd, her staying at home with the servants? I thought she'd go to London with her father.

Christine   'Spect she doesn't want to bump into anyone she knows. It's embarrassing for a lady to be jilted like that.

Pause.

John   I was there. When he gave her the elbow.

Christine (*interested*)   Really?

John   My natural discretion forbids me to gossip.

Christine   Suit yourself.

John   They were down at the stables, 'horsing around'. She was mucking about with this whip, 'training him' she said. She was getting him to jump over it, like a dog. He does it twice and each time she gives him a whack. Third time he goes nuts and lashes out with the back of his hand – his ring cut her. Then he takes the whip and breaks it, her heart 'n'all.

Christine   And what were *you* doing 'down at the stables'?

John   Just . . . idling. Something smells good . . .

Christine   Kidneys on toast.

She serves him the food.

John   You can't beat a kidney – 'specially the black market variety.

He gives her a playful little smack.

You might've warmed the plate.

Christine   You're worse than his Lordship with your fussing.

He begins to eat. She strokes his hair and kisses his neck.

John   Don't confuse my appetites.

She strokes his cheek.

Christine   Bit rough . . .

John   My razor's broken. Will you get us a new one?

Christine   Anything for his Lordship.

John   You can have a lend.

Christine   Don't be rude.

She puts a bottle of beer on the table for him.

John   Beer?! We're supposed to be celebrating.

He fetches an already opened bottle of red wine.

His Lordship's best Burgundy. Off the table last night.

Christine *hands him a straight glass.*

John   *Wine* glass . . .

Christine   Isn't he particular? Heaven help the woman
who marries you.

She hands him a wine glass.

John   Easy, you're talking to a gentleman here. *Your*
gentleman, perhaps.

He tastes the wine ostentatiously to amuse her.

Like Winston Churchill: robust, full-bodied . . .

He drains the glass.

And finished.

Christine   Poor Winston.

John   Hardly *poor*.

She puts a pan on the stove and begins to stir.

I remember buying crates of this, with his Lordship, before the war . . .

Pause. John continues to eat and read his newspaper.

After a while he detects the smell from **Christine**'s *pan, it disturbs him.*

What's the stench?

Christine   A magic potion. Miss Julie wants it for Emily.

John   Cooking for her mutt? You're s'posed to have the night off. (*ironic*) 'It's a scandal!'

Christine   Poor dog's up the duff, gatekeeper's pug gave it a seeing to. Miss Julie's livid.

John   So what's with the brew?

She mimes that the potion will induce a miscarriage.

No!

Christine   Honest! She says the dog's betrayed her.

John   She's off her rocker!

He hands her his plate.

Thanks, love. (*mocking*) The aristocracy just *adore* the animals – that's why they hunt them. We kill what we love.

He starts to polish the shoes.

Her mother was a madwoman too. D'you remember her sitting in here? What did she call it – 'fraternising with the troops.' (*shaking his head*) No wonder they're a dying breed. Miss Julie's supposed to be the lady of the house but you should've seen her in the barn gallivanting with the gardeners, even the stable lads got their turn.

Christine   And the chauffeur.

John   That's different, I'm –

Christine   What?

John Just different. The rich should never sell themselves cheap. They try to act common they become common. She dances well though, I'll give her that.

Christine That's not all you'll give her.

John Oi! Respect for your betters, girl! She's a fine-looking filly though. Good skin . . . and . . . et cetera.

Christine You'd be surprised, Claire dresses her and she told me –

John Ah, the jealousy of women.

A number finishes outside. Applause.

Christine Will you dance with me when I've done this?

John Course.

Christine Promise?

John I just said I would.

Miss Julie *enters and stands in the doorway. She is flushed from dancing and a little too much alcohol.*

John *conceals the wine bottle and rises respectfully, slipping on his jacket and standing almost to attention.* **Christine** *stands by the stove, likewise.*

Pause.

Julie Good evening, John. Again.

John Good Evening, Miss Julie.

Julie Is it ready, Christine?

Christine Nearly, Miss.

Julie Will you be an angel and pour it into a bottle?

Christine Yes, Miss Julie.

Miss Julie *enters and wanders around.* **John** *and* **Christine** *remain stationary.*

Julie   Are you both overcome with excitement?

They don't know what she means.

The election!

Christine   Yes, Miss.

Julie   I take it you did both vote for The Labour Party?

Christine   Yes, Miss Julie.

She continues with her work at the stove.

Julie   And you, John?

John   Secret ballot, Miss, I'm afraid I can't reveal.

She flips him in the face with her handkerchief.

Julie   Impertinence!

John (*breathes in*)   Violet.

Julie   Sense of smell *and* rhythm, where does his talent end?

She offers her arm.

Shall we?

Pause.

John   No offence meant, Miss Julie, but I did promise this one with Christine.

Miss Julie *is disappointed but tries not to show it.*

Julie   *To* Christine. She can dance with you any time – can't you, Christine? I command you to lend me this man!

Christine   It's fine, I've got to finish this. (*Urges him.*) Go on, John . . .

John   I don't mean to be rude but is it proper for you to dance twice in one night with me? People will talk.

Julie   What people? What 'talk'?

John   I'm not sure you should favour one member of the staff as opposed to another.

Julie   You're doing *me* the favour. I can dance with who I like as often as I like whenever I like. We're a free country now, John. I know, you're a secret Tory, aren't you? Everyone in their place forever.

John   No, Miss Julie.

Julie   And stop calling me 'Miss'.

She hits him with her handkerchief again.

Just for tonight? We can go back to the dark ages tomorrow if you'd prefer. Come on, dance with me! I like the way you lead. All the other men are positively club-footed.

John   As you wish, I'm at your service.

Julie   It's not an order, it's an invitation! Erase that face of feudal anxiety and come and dance!

She leads him outside.

The music strikes up.

Christine *washes up* **John***'s plate.*

She puts the wine bottle away.

She puts the 'potion' bottle on the table ready for **Miss Julie***.*

She removes her apron and hangs it on a hook by her desk.

John*'s suit is hanging up, she removes a speck of dust from it and lays it ready for him on the table.*

She notices that **Miss Julie** *has left her handkerchief and bag. She carefully folds the handkerchief and places it with the bag next to the potion bottle.*

She sits at her desk, tired. She yawns, stretches a little. Then she takes a hand mirror and make-up from a drawer and applies lipstick and powder.

She looks at herself. Lights a cigarette, smokes, closes her eyes, exhausted.

She listens to the music. Waiting for **John** *to return.*

She eases back in her chair, trying to get comfortable. She rests her head on her arms on the desk.

Her cigarette smoulders in the ashtray. She falls asleep.

After a while the number ends. Applause.

Presently, **John** *enters.*

He sees that she's asleep and gently stubs out the cigarette.

He goes to the sink and washes his face. It is a hot night and he is sweating from dancing.

Christine *wakes up, watches him.*

John   She's mad all right. Everyone was laughing at her. She was cavorting like a woman possessed!

Christine   Don't be mean, she's not herself. She's got the curse this week, Claire told me.

John *laughs. A new number strikes up.*

This one's mine.

She puts her arms round his neck and they begin to sway to the distant music. Their faces are close.

John   You're not angry with me, for going off?

Christine   You had to. I know my place and I think that you do too.

John   You are going to make a – very – good – wife.

On each word he kisses her. They are locked in embrace as **Miss Julie** *enters.* **Christine** *has her back to* **Miss Julie**. **John** *faces her. They stare at each other. Then he gently disengages himself.*

Julie   Please, carry on . . .

Christine   The medicine's ready, Miss, for Emily.

Julie   So I see. (*To* **John**.) You're a charming partner, running away from your lady like that.

John   On the contrary, Miss, I've run *to* her.

Julie   Hold on tight to this one, Christine. He's an incomparable dancer but slippery.

Pause. She comes further into the room.

(*To* **John**.) Why are you wearing your uniform? Take it off, you're not working tonight.

John   I haven't had time to change, Miss Julie, I drove his Lordship up to town.

Julie   I know. Is this your suit?

John   Yes.

Julie   Put it on, it's nice.

He hesitates. She issues an order, slowly, seductively.

Put it on, John.

John   Will you excuse me, my Lady?

Julie   Don't mind me, I'll cover my eyes.

John *and* **Christine** *are shocked and a little embarrassed.*

John   With your permission I'll go to my room, Miss.

Julie   As you wish.

He exits with his suit. Pause.

Miss Julie *takes out her cigarette case from her clutch bag.*

Christine   Here you are, Miss.

She gives **Miss Julie** *a light.*

Julie   Thank you. Would you like one?

Christine   No thank you, Miss.

Pause.

Julie   Don't mind me if you have work to do.

Christine   Thank you, Miss.

Christine *sits at her desk and goes through some paperwork. Pause.*

Julie   Is John your fiancé? You seem quite . . . intimate?

Christine   We were going to marry but then the war came and . . . we're not engaged officially.

Julie   Officially?

Christine   Well, I don't have a ring, Miss.

Pause.

Julie (*to herself*)   I had a ring . . .

Christine *stifles a yawn.*

Julie   I'm sorry, Christine, am I boring you?

Christine   No, Miss Julie, I'm very sorry, I'm tired.

Julie   Then you must go to bed.

Christine   John promised me a dance, I'll just –

Julie   Men like to keep their women, not their promises.

Miss Julie *smokes. After a while* **John** *returns in his suit. During the next sequence of dialogue* **Christine** *falls asleep again.*

Julie   *Très gentil, Monsieur Jean, très gentil.*

John   *Vous voulez plaisanter, Mademoiselle.*

Julie   *Et vous voulez parler français.* Where did you learn that?

John   I picked up a bit during the war, in France.

Julie   I hope that's all you picked up in France.

The joke falls flat.

You look quite the gentleman in that suit. *Charmant.*

John   You flatter me.

Julie   Flatter you?

John   My position forbids me to believe that you would pay me an authentic compliment and therefore I must assume that you were exaggerating your praise . . . or flattering.

Julie   My, what language! Are you a patron of the theatre?

John   I used to accompany his Lordship sometimes. And on his travels abroad too.

Julie   But you grew up here, didn't you?

John   My father was a labourer on the estate. Our family's worked here for centuries.

Pause.

I remember you as a child . . .

Julie   Really? What do you remember?

*He nods to **Christine** who is now asleep.*

Julie   *(whispering)*   She's asleep . . .

They watch her.

Do you think she snores?

Pause.

John   No.

Pause.

She talks.

*They look at each other. **Miss Julie** nervously reaches for another cigarette.*

Julie   Smoke?

John   No, thank you.

Julie   Do you have a light?

He quietly takes **Christine***'s matches from her desk and lights* **Miss Julie***'s cigarette.*

Merci, Monsieur. Why don't you smoke? I thought all soldiers smoked?

John   I'm not a soldier anymore.

Julie   You have a weak chest. Yes, my father told me. You were demobbed two months early . . . for your weak chest.

John   Yes.

Julie   Why don't you sit down?

John   I wouldn't take such a liberty in your presence.

Julie   But if I ordered you?

John   Then I'd obey.

Julie   Then sit.

As he is about to sit.

No, wait, have you anything to drink?

John   Only beer.

Julie   'Only'? I like beer. I'm just a simple country girl, John.

He fetches a bottle of beer and pours her a glass.

Julie   What was the war like?

John   Like? Like nothing.

Julie   Did you kill lots of Germans?

John   Hundreds.

Julie   Not thousands?

John   Hundreds of thousands.

He serves her the glass of beer.

Julie   Thank you. Won't you keep me company?

John   I'm not really a beer drinker but if my Ladyship commands . . .

Julie   Courtesy commands, John.

As he pours himself a glass she lies back on a bench.

Do you think I'm a dreadful lush?

John   No, my Lady.

Julie   *I* think I'm a dreadful lush. Now, a toast . . . to me.

John   To you.

Julie   To you.

John   To me.

Julie   To Socialism.

John   To Socialism.

Julie   To peace.

John   To peace.

Julie   What else? To Love.

John   To Love.

Julie   To the workers.

John   The workers.

Julie   Bravo.

They drink.

Now kiss my shoe.

He stares at her.

As a sign of respect.

She dangles her foot.

Pause.

He moves to her, she snatches her foot away.

Pause. They look at each other.

She dangles her foot. He moves to her. She snatches it away.

He stares at her. She dangles her foot. He moves very fast, catches it, holds it.

They look at each other.

He kneels and kisses her shoe.

Very good. Too quick for me, Monsieur Jean.

He straightens up.

John   I think we'd better drink up, Miss Julie. Someone might see us.

Julie   Close the shutters.

John   Everyone was talking out there before . . .

Julie   What were they saying?

John   They were being . . . suggestive. You know what I mean, you're not a child. If they see you in here at night, drinking, alone . . .

Julie   We're not alone, your wife-to-be is with us.

John   Asleep.

Julie   Then I'll wake her.

She looks at him and then saunters over to **Christine**.

Christine! Christine!

(*To* **John**.) Dead to the world . . .

Christine! Wake up! Protect us from gossip!

John (*sharp*)   Leave her alone.

Miss Julie *turns to him, a little shocked by his tone but pleased he prevented her from waking* **Christine**.

John   She's been working all day, she's exhausted. Let her sleep.

Julie   A noble sentiment, it does you credit.

She faces him.

Come outside and pick some lilacs for me.

John   I can't. It's not possible.

Julie   Why?

John   Them.

He gestures outside.

Julie   They think I could fall for a servant?

John   They know no better.

Julie   You're a snob! I have a higher opinion of 'them' than you. Come.

John   You're welcome to your opinions. I know these people. They don't see what's there, they see what's in their heads.

Julie   Well, let's find out. *Come.*

She faces him, hands outstretched.

John (*softly*)   You're strange . . .

Julie   Everything's strange . . . life . . . people . . . everything's a scum that drifts across the water until it sinks.

Pause.

Come with me. What does it matter what people say or think?

He thinks. Moves towards her. He stops, rubs his eye.

Julie   What's wrong?

John   Nothing, dust.

Julie   Let me see.

She sits him down and tilts his head back. She gently pushes his eyelid up to look.

Christine *has awoken but is still sleepy* . . .

Keep still . . . don't flinch . . . I can feel you flinching . . .
keep . . . still . . . it's a lash . . . a long black lash . . .

Christine   What's the matter?

John   Nothing, just a lash.

Christine   He's squeamish about his eyes. May I, Miss?

Miss Julie *moves to one side.*

John   I'm fine, it's gone.

Christine   Let me look.

John   It's gone.

Pause.

Christine   You left your bag, Miss, and the medicine's
there for Emily.

Julie   Thank you.

Pause. **Miss Julie** *shows no sign of leaving.*

Christine   Do you need me for anything, Miss?

Julie   No, I'm fine. Thank you, Christine.

Christine   Then if you'll excuse me, I'll go to bed, Miss.

Julie   Of course.

Christine   Goodnight, Miss Julie.

Julie   Goodnight, Christine.

John   Goodnight.

Christine *hovers, a little awkwardly.*

Christine   Shall I get you up, for church?

John   Thank you.

Christine   Goodnight, Miss.

Christine *exits.* **John** *busies himself, tidying up.*

Julie   Where were we?

John   You were telling me your theory of life.

Julie   Don't be cruel.

Silence. They become conscious of the music outside.

Julie   Tell me about your visits to the theatre, with my father.

John   There's not much to tell. I used to drive him to the theatre, he would sit in the royal circle, I in the Gods. After the performance he would dine at his club, I would wait in the car.

Julie   What would you do, 'in the car'?

John   Read the paper, the programme, talk to the other chauffeurs . . . in their cars.

Julie   Never any women?

John   Women chauffeurs? Hardly.

Julie   Did you talk to any women? Prostitutes?

John   No.

Julie   Did my father talk to any women?

John   No.

Julie   Pros–

John   No.

Julie   My mother died ten years ago, what's a man to do?

John   What indeed.

Julie   Do I shock you?

John   Not as much as you'd like to.

Pause.

Julie   And would you discuss the play on the way home?

John   Sometimes.

Julie   Are those his shoes?

John   Yes.

Julie   Do you like my father?

John   Yes.

Julie   But do you respect him?

John   Yes.

Julie   Because he got you home from the war?

Pause.

John   Yes.

Julie   Do you wish he were *your* father?

Silence. They are close.

I'm sorry, that wasn't a very grown-up question.

John   You're only young . . .

Julie   And so innocent . . .

John   I think not . . .

Julie   It's true . . . Monsieur Jean . . .

She gazes at him.

He moves to kiss her.

She slaps him hard on the cheek.

Pause.

John   I have work to do, it's way past your bedtime, I suggest you retire.

Julie (*amused*)   What work?

John *starts polishing a shoe.*

Julie   Put it down.

He ignores her.

PUT IT DOWN!

He puts the shoe down.

You're *proud*. You're a Don Juan – a Don John. Have you ever been to the opera?

John   No.

Julie   When Covent Garden re-opens I will take you. But unlike my hypocrite father you will sit with me in the grand tier. Would you like that?

John   I have to clean these shoes for the morning. It's not my job to amuse you.

Julie   Please don't sulk.

Silence.

Well, goodnight then.

She stubs out her cigarette, leaves her clutch bag on the table and heads for the door. She hovers there.

Pause.

John   You've forgotten your bag.

Julie   Well, bring it to me then.

John *rises and hands her the bag.*

Julie   Thank you, John. Goodnight.

John   Goodnight, Miss Julie.

They face each other.

Silence. She heads back into the room.

Julie   Do you love Christine very much?

John   Of course.

Julie   But are you *in* love with her, there's a difference isn't there? I'm not sure I've ever been in love. What about you? Have you ever been in love, John? Sick with love?

Pause.

John   Only as a child.

Julie   Who was she?

Pause.

John   You know who.

He looks down.

Ridiculous, isn't it?

Julie   No. Tell me . . .

John   I'd been in your father's orchard . . . his 'Garden of Eden' . . . I'd decided to steal some apples . . .

Julie   Scrumping.

John   Stealing. I was with my mother, weeding your onion beds, in the field out where the barn is now.

Julie   I thought the barn was always there?

John   No, it was built when you were seven. Those who work the land know it better than those who own it.

Julie   You're a red!

John   Far from it.

Julie   A cynic then.

John   Realist. It was the summer of '27 . . . I was twelve . . . I left my mother to it, thought I'd sneak into the orchard and go 'scrumping'. I climbed a tree, dropped down and found myself in a garden party – uninvited – everyone in their finery – your mother – it was a summer evening, like tonight . . . I was in rags – I was scared so I ran and I fell in the slurry pit, I got covered in shit (sorry) – and I ran and ran 'til I ended up on the other side of the lake facing the stables where it's boarded up now . . .

Julie   I know.

John   And I saw a white dress with a pink ribbon . . .

Julie   Here . . .

She gestures to her throat.

John   Yes. And the girl in the white dress was patting a black pony. I lay in the brambles, I couldn't move or they'd cut me and I watched the girl stroking the animal and I could see the girl was whispering to it, whispering all her secrets. And she looked sad and alone. And I fell in love with you.

Julie   I wasn't sad, I was happy. I wanted to die.

John   Why?

Julie   Because I was so happy.

John   But that's not when it started. When I was five . . . I saw your mother pushing you in your pram . . . a blue black pram . . . your carriage. I was five and could already feel the difference between us. My first memory is *you* . . . and a feeling without the words to describe it. Now I can call it love . . . or envy. A man of my class can rise, like bread, but not cake.

Julie   But the world is changing . . .

John   Not biology.

Julie   But there are such opportunities now, for self-improvement . . .

John   I'm a self made man if that's what you mean. Your father's been good to me, lending me books. You can learn a lot by observation.

Julie   And do you still observe *me*? What do you see?

John Just things. You can be quite a coarse young lady, can't you?

Julie Whatever do you mean?

John Maybe we're not so different; you, me, Christine . . . your officer friend.

Julie *We* never slept together.

John No, but you wanted to.

Julie Nonsense. He wanted to, I refused.

John That's not what I heard . . . and saw.

Pause.

Julie When?

John Two weeks ago, the stables.

Julie What a little Peeping John you are. I could have you dismissed for spying on me. I could tell my father and –

John I would have to tell him what I saw: his daughter on her knees unbuttoning the officer's britches.

Julie Nothing happened.

John I know, you scared him off. God knows why they decorated *him* for bravery.

Julie (*furious*) That's enough, this conversation is over.

She heads for the door.

John Fine, have I your permission to go to bed?

Julie With Christine?

John Who knows?

Pause.

Julie Where are the keys to the boathouse?

John Over there.

Julie   Row me out to the lake, I want to see the moon.

John   Look out the window.

Pause.

Julie (*realises*)   You're afraid for *your* reputation.

John   Maybe. If anyone suspected I'd be dismissed without a reference, just as I'm getting on. I also have a duty to Christine.

Julie   Ah, Christine!

John   And you – and your father who trusts me. You play with fire, Miss Julie.

Julie   Lucky I'm insured.

The last number ends outside. Applause.

John   You're tired and drunk, it makes you rash. You'd regret everything in the morning.

Julie   Regret what?

John   Don't play the innocent.

Julie   I *am* innocent, I told you . . . I'm not –

John   Go to bed.

Sound of a drunken crowd approaching from outside.

Go now, they're coming!

He quickly extinguishes the lights. He bolts the door and closes the shutters.

The crowd are outside the kitchen. Loud.

The room is now lit by a single remaining lamp.

Please, Miss Julie, obey me this once, go now!

Julie   Me? Obey you?

John   Yes.

Julie   And if I don't?

The sound outside intensifies, the room seems to be surrounded.

Julie   No way out!

Someone tries the lock. The crowd are singing now. **Miss Julie** *and* **John** *huddle together.*

Julie   Don't be scared. What are they singing?

John   An obscene song about you and me.

Julie   They wouldn't dare.

John   You think they respect you? They're drunk, they're a rabble, they laugh at you, to them you're . . . just . . . mad.

Julie   But I'm *nice* to everyone.

John   You think you're being nice but you're being patronising. You can't help it, it's in your blood.

They kiss and begin to struggle with each other's clothes – aggressive, laughing, scared.

Julie   Take me to your room.

She whispers, intimately.

John   What?

Julie   Just take me to your room.

The banging on the doors and windows increases.

John *and* **Miss Julie** *exit hurriedly.*

Fade.

Later. About five in the morning, grey half-light.

The single lamp remains lit. The shutters are closed.

Christine *enters doing up her dressing gown.*

She heads to her desk, finds a cigarette and lights it. She smokes. She pockets her pack of cigarettes.

She goes to the sink and has a sip of water.

She looks for an ashtray and finds one on the table. She stares at it.

She sees the beer glasses, one with lipstick on the rim.

She sees **Miss Julie**'s *bag and the potion bottle are still on the table.*

She thinks, takes a drag, leaves her cigarette smouldering in the ashtray.

She exits in the direction of **John**'s *room.*

Thirty seconds.

Christine *comes back, distraught.*

She heads back towards her room. Remembers. Returns and picks up her cigarette, takes a drag, stubs it out, unfinished.

She exits.

Fade.

Later. Dawn. Morning light through the cracks in the shutters.

Miss Julie *enters, hair down, smeared make-up, tired. She carries her shoes.*

She goes to her cigarette case on the table but it is empty.

She goes to the sink, washes her face, drinks from her hands.

There is a small patch of blood on her dress. She takes a rag and rubs at the dress.

John *enters in trousers and loose shirt, no shoes. He watches her. She sees him, holds up the bloodied rag.*

Julie   Where . . . ?

John   Here . . .

He sees the blood on the rag.

Julie   Sorry.

He takes the rag and puts it in the bin.

John   You all right?

She nods. They kiss, tenderly.

Silence. Exchange of looks.

John   You're all right?

Julie   Mmmhm.

He offers her a chair, she sits.

Julie   Are there any cigarettes around?

John *searches* **Christine**'s *desk.*

John   'Fraid not.

Miss Julie *spots a half-smoked butt in the ashtray. She extracts it happily.* **John** *grins and fetches her a light. She strokes his hand as he offers the flame.*

Julie   *Merci, ma chérie.*

John   *Mon plaisir.*

He sits with her as she smokes.

So . . . New York. That's the place for us. Yeah? New life, new people. I met some GI's during the war, I got their addresses, everything. They live in . . . the Bronx. We'll have to look them up. Maybe they'll help us with the night-club? I imagine it'll be very English, glamorous, sophisticated. They love us over there, they die for the accent. I'll do the books, the bar . . . you'll be front of house, charm everyone . . .

Miss Julie *nods, smiles.*

Have to hurry though, Christine'll be up soon and your father's due back. I'll drive us to the station, we'll catch the train, on the boat . . . we're there. How long does it take? Two, three days?

Julie   A week.

John   A week.

Julie   Tell me you love me.

John   I love you.

Julie   Come here.

He kisses her.

John   We have to go, Miss Julie.

Julie   How can you call me *Miss* now?!

John   Because we're *here* . . . in this house with your father's shoes waiting to be cleaned. And me sitting here full of respect . . . that bell rings – I jump. But in America it'll be different . . . I won't feel suffocated . . . I'll be rich.

Julie   I don't care if you're rich. Tell me you love me.

John   I love you.

They kiss.

Come on, be practical. New York, the nightclub, what do you think?

Julie   It sounds fine but a business requires capital, do you have any?

John   Of course: experience, expertise, nous – that's capital of a sort.

Julie   It won't buy you a railway ticket.

John   So . . . we need a backer . . .

Pause.

Julie   John, I don't have any money. I don't have a bean. It's all in . . . trust.

Long silence.

John   Oh well . . .

Julie   What . . . ?

John   We stay here.

Julie   I can't stay here . . . as your mistress. My father –
people – we can't stay here, surely you see that?

John (*cold*)   I don't see anything.

Julie   But we won't need money, we'll be together.

John   We need money to *be* together.

Silence.

Julie   What have I done?

John   Fallen . . . briefly . . . but pleasurably, I trust.

Julie   You hate me . . . ?

John   No.

Julie   You took advantage of me?

John   Vice versa, I think.

Julie   But you just said you loved me . . . ?

John   You confuse love and desire.

Julie   I love *you*.

John   Congratulations.

Julie   How can you . . . what *are* you?

John   Just a man. Stop acting the weeping debutante, Miss
Julie. We had a roll in the hay, forget it, have a drink, you're
more fun when you're tight.

Julie   You owe me respect at least.

John   That's the last thing you wanted in there. Do you
know, you actually shocked me.

Julie   You're disgusting.

John   No, *you're* disgusting. I told you it would end in tears.
I have work to do.

He starts polishing the shoes.

Isn't this where we started?

Julie But the things you said . . . ? What about your story? The white dress, the pony . . . ?

John I told you what you wanted to hear, it's called seduction.

Julie Am I your conquest? Nothing more?

John Don't force me to be cruel.

Julie Tell me what I am.

Pause.

John A fuck.

Julie (*childlike, to herself*) I'm all dirty.

John So wash.

Julie STAND UP WHEN YOU SPEAK TO ME! STAND UP! REMEMBER YOUR POSITION!

He stands.

John Which one, Madame? There were so many.

Julie You're still a servant, you scared little squaddie, you're still a servant.

John And you're a servant's slut. Don't come on all superior with me, Miss Julie. No woman of my class would accost me the way you did last night, no woman of my class would want what you wanted last night; sweating and braying, your face in the pillow, biting your hand to stop yourself screaming the house down. You'd shame a two-bit tart in Piccadilly.

Julie Do I deserve this?

John What's a man to think if you beg him to beat you?

She breaks down.

Julie   Please no more . . . I know . . . I'm bad . . . I'm a bad girl.

He puts his arms round her, full of pity and desire.

John   No you're not . . . I'm as much to blame . . . I didn't mean what I said . . . please, I'm sorry . . .

Julie   Hurt me again.

John   You mustn't say that, things just . . . went too far. No one knows, you must try to forget about it.

Julie   Did you love me? At least in bed?

John   Of course I did, couldn't you tell?

Julie   How could I? I have no experience, I haven't lived.

John   Come on, you're being –

Julie   DON'T TELL ME WHAT I'M BEING!

Beat.

Do I look ugly?

He stares at her.

Is this what you wanted? Me – reduced? Is this your revenge? Your little class victory?

John   No. I've dreamt about you all my life . . . and now I have to wake up. I'm not saying I couldn't love you, of course I could . . . I only have to look at you . . . you're gorgeous.

He tries to kiss her.

Julie   Get off! GET YOUR HANDS OFF ME! What kind of a man is excited by a woman's despair?

John   Any man, I imagine.

She paces round the kitchen, almost oblivious to him.

Julie   I must run away. I can't stay here, I could never live it down and when my father finds out he'll kill me. He plays

the Labour peer but he despises the lower classes, they're
too stupid and disappointing. He'd sack you on the spot and
make my life a misery. And I won't be a laughing stock for
the servants – you say they find me condescending?

John Patronising.

Julie Shut up, I'm trying to think. Give me a drink.

He fetches the wine bottle and a glass.

Come on! Come on! JUMP!

*He pours her a glass and she gulps it down. She holds out the glass for
more.*

John You've had enough.

Julie No such thing. POUR.

He does so.

God I want a cigarette, where the hell are Christine's?

John No idea.

Julie I don't regret anything. Everything's just dandy. I'll
run away just like the pictures –

John Miss Julie –

Julie Shut up! Have you seen that one with . . . I've lost
my thought . . . did I tell you about my mother? She had
this thing about women's emancipation . . . she swore she'd
never marry so she told my father she would be his lover but
never his wife.

Pause.

But then . . . I was born. I was . . . a mistake, really.

John You're illegitimate?

Julie Mmm, funny isn't it? So they had to get married
and my mother brought me up as . . . a child of nature. She
wanted me to demonstrate the equality of the sexes. She

used to dress me up in boy's clothes and made me learn about farming – she made me kill a fox when I was . . .

She pauses briefly, remembering.

And then she reorganised the estate, the women had to do the men's work and the men the women's. We were the laughing stock of the whole county. Finally, my father snapped and she fell into line. But she began to stay out all night . . . she took lovers, people talked, she blamed my father for the failure of her experiment . . . her infidelities were her revenge. They rowed constantly, and fought, she often had terrible gashes and bruises . . . he did too, she was very strong when she was angry . . . and then there was a rumour that my father tried to kill himself . . .

John *is stunned.*

Yes, he failed . . . (*Smiles.*) obviously.

Pause.

I didn't know whose side I was on . . . I think I learnt all my emotions by the age of ten and never developed any more. (*Softly.*) A child experiences the world so deeply . . . without the sophistication to protect itself . . . it's not fair really.

Pause.

My mother – almost on her deathbed – no, *on* her deathbed, made me swear that I'd never be a slave to any man.

John   And the Officer?

Julie   He was to be *my* slave.

John   But he did a runner.

Julie   It was more complicated than that.

John   Didn't look like it.

Julie   From your vantage point probably not. How can *you* see? You watch the world through eyes filled with acid.

John   You hate me too?

Julie   Of course.

John   But not when I was inside you.

Julie   I was weak, I won't be again. If it were up to me I'd have you shot and fed to the dogs, like a fallen horse at the Grand National.

John   Only thoroughbreds run the National.

Julie   They let the odd nag in, ones with weak chests, *'pour encourager les autres.'*

He grabs hold of her and forces her down on the table, head first.

You wouldn't dare!

He pulls up her dress.

Supposing your sow squeals for her pig? Supposing Daddy rings his bell?

He lets her go.

The truth is, I must bolt. Enjoy myself for a couple of days, a week if I can stand myself that long and then . . .

She gestures across her throat, unseen by him.

John   New York sounds more attractive.

Julie   You?! In the capital of the world?! You wouldn't survive five minutes! You, with your clumsy hands and grubby nails, your quick wit but slow, slow mind. Your pub talk and your pools and the way you swill your beer like a mouthwash. You wouldn't suit New York – in your ill-fitting suit – your demob disaster – hacked together by some gnarled troll in the East End. You? Run a nightclub? I remember you at the village fair, you couldn't even run the egg-and-spoon race because of your 'weak chest'!

John   At last, the true blue blood speaks! The little blue-blooded bastard! And you called *me* a snob? I read up on your 'pedigree' once, that book in your father's study. (*Glances up.*) Would you like to know who your earliest ancestor was? A farmer, a stinking, stupid farmer and five hundred years ago he pimped his wife to the king. And in return . . . all this. Doubtless she enjoyed it, the slag. The blood of a whore runs through you for centuries.

He holds her face. They stare at each other.

Julie   Die with me John, a suicide pact.

John   Suicide's for cowards.

Julie   Chicken.

John   It's a crime against God's law.

Julie   You believe in God?

John   Passionately. I'm in love with the bloke.

He breaks free of her.

I'm going to bed.

He starts to exit.

Julie   You forget who I am.

He stops.

John   Oh yeah, sorry.

He takes some loose change from his pocket and throws it on the table.

John   Cheers, darling.

Julie (*calm*)   Not enough. You take my virginity, you humiliate me, you abuse me and my family's honour – there's a *price*. You don't leave this room. You listen to what I say or help me God I will scream rape and I will not stop screaming until you are in prison.

John   Miss Julie . . . I'm sorry. I'm sorry I've hurt you. I know you're suffering, I'm sorry for that, truly. But I'm to be married. This is where I belong and so do you. In time you'll forget about this until it's just a dull ache. You'll live with it, that's life.

Julie   Pain hurts, I won't tolerate it.

John   You have to.

Pause.

Julie   Why don't you love me?

John   I do.

Julie   No. Why *can't* you love me?

Pause.

John   Fear.

Pause.

Julie   John . . . tell me what to do. Order me. I'm so tired I can't think. My legs feel hollowed out, as if I've no blood.

John   Go upstairs. Get dressed. Get money for the journey – from your father's desk, second drawer down, the key's on the mantelpiece under the clock.

Julie   Come with me.

John   I can't.

Julie   No, to my room.

He hesitates.

John   I can't.

Julie   Please.

John   Go. Come down when you're ready, I'll drive you to the station.

Julie   Be nice to me.

John   Orders never sound nice. Now you know. *Go.*

She exits.

John *opens the shutters and begins to 'normalise' the room: he pockets his change, bins the dog medicine, hides the clutch bag, empties the* *ashtray, clears the bottle and glass, removes the rag from the bin and manages to slip it into his pocket as* **Christine** *enters.*

She's dressed for church. She carries a suit, shirt and tie on a hanger.

Christine   Morning.

John   Morning, love.

Christine   I gave these a press, for church.

She hands him his clothes.

John   Cheers. Won't be a minute.

He goes to exit.

Christine   No one's up, get dressed in here.

John   In here?

Christine   Hurry up, we'll be late.

He starts to get changed. **Christine** *sits and observes him. Silence.*

John   What's the lesson today?

Christine   I don't know. You look tired.

John   Nightmares, the usual. You slept all right?

Christine   Like a log.

He's struggling with his tie a little.

John   Will you do this?

She ties his tie. He strokes her cheek. She catches his hand and smells his fingers.

Christine   These need a wash.

They look at each other. Suddenly she slaps him hard on the cheek. He stares at her.

Christine   I woke in the night, I opened your door.

Pause.

You both had your backs to me.

Pause.

I was wondering if you'd tell me, since we are to be married, for better or worse.

John   Course I'd've told you. I'm sorry.

Christine   Don't bother. I imagine you did it with every little scrubber in France. I have low expectations, I'm rarely disappointed. I understand, how could you resist her beauty when you're just a man?

She slaps him again.

We're not staying here by the way, so you can forget it ever happening again. I'm not working in a house where I can't respect my superiors.

John   There's more to life than respecting superiors.

Christine (*furiously*)   You hypocrite, you cringe before his Lordship. I've seen you; reading his books, trying to engage him in 'political conversation'. You bore him, he thinks you're a crawler.

Beat.

I'm surprised at her though, had it been a gentleman, I could understand it, but *you* . . . who are you?

John   It wasn't her fault, I took advantage.

Christine   Ah, defending his mistress's honour, how noble.

Pause.

What was she like?

John   Christine –

Christine   No, don't tell me, I saw.

Beat.

Your rash is getting worse.

Beat.

Look at you, you can't believe it, can you? You're still reliving it in your head, your dirty little film in your dirty little fleapit of a mind.

John   You've made your point.

Christine   We'll hand in our notice today. We'll stay with my sister while we get sorted. You can find work as a porter or a caretaker. Somewhere steady and secure with a good pension for a wife. And children. We'll be wanting to start a family as soon as we're married. Won't we?

John   Yes.

A door slams overhead in the study.

Christine   Who's that?

John   Claire, probably.

Christine   Could it be his Lordship? Home early? He might've got the first train?

John   No, he'd have telephoned.

Christine   Well, he might be about to – have you done his shoes?

John   Nearly.

Christine   I'll make his coffee.

John   I'll do it. You don't want to be late for church, I'll catch you up on the way. Go on . . . it's fine . . . I'll serve him his coffee, have a shave and then . . .

Christine   What?

He can't speak. He's decided to run away with **Miss Julie**.

What?

John   I've just got things . . . to do.

Christine   Fine. I'll wait for you at the gate.

John   The gate.

Christine   At the end of the drive.

John   I know.

Christine *exits.* **John** *paces, working it out, excited.*

After a while, **Miss Julie** *enters dressed to travel. She carries a suitcase, bag, hatbox and a birdcage covered with a cloth.* **John** *helps her.*

Julie   I saw Christine going out.

John   She's off to Mass.

He gazes at her.

Julie   Does she suspect?

John   No, nothing. You look . . . so beautiful.

Julie   Do I?

John   Yes.

She opens her case and takes out a child's white dress with a pink ribbon.

Julie   Look. My dress. It was in the nursery.

She holds it against herself. He caresses her.

Julie   Come with me. There was a fortune in Daddy's desk. Come with me, wherever you want, don't leave me alone.

John   Show me.

Julie   It's in my bag.

He takes out a huge wad of notes. Stares at them in amazement.

John   It would take me five years to earn this.

Pause.

Fine. Let's go. But *now*!

Julie   I'm ready!

He puts on his jacket, she helps him.

John   We have to go now!

Julie   I'm ready! You haven't got any shoes on!

John   I'll get some.

She gestures to her father's shoes.

Julie   Wear those.

He hesitates. She insists now.

Put them on . . .

He hesitates.

Put them on, John.

He thinks then puts them on, she watches him intently.

John   And no luggage, it's a giveaway.

Julie   Yes, only what we can take in the compartment.

He notices the birdcage.

John   What's that?

She removes the cloth.

Julie   It's Serena, she's mine. I can't leave her here.

John   Don't be ridiculous, we can't take that!

Julie   Don't be cruel, let me take her!

John   Put it down. Put the cage down! Put – the cage – down!

Julie   DON'T ORDER ME!

John   Shh! Your father might be back any minute – Christine – anyone. Give me the cage.

Julie   I'm not leaving her here. Let's set her free.

John   It's a house bird, it wouldn't survive a day out there.

Julie   Then kill her.

Pause.

Are you scared?

John   No.

She takes the bird out of the cage.

Julie   Please don't let her suffer.

She stares at the bird.

Must you die and leave your mistress behind?

*She gives **John** the bird. He takes it over to the chopping block.*

John   Please, no scenes. It's a dumb animal. I'm going to kill it and then we'll go . . . understand . . . I suggest you look away . . . UNDERSTAND.

She nods. He looks around for the hatchet. She hands him the bread knife.

He looks away. She stares, transfixed.

Julie (*quietly*)   Don't . . .

He cuts the bird's head off.

He wipes the blade on a rag.

There's blood between us.

John   Let's go.

Julie   Go? With you? Now?

She picks up the decapitated bird and smears blood from it onto his face.

Who's scared of blood? Who's scared of blood? Tell me, who's scared of blood?

She kisses him aggressively then thrusts her hand into his trousers.

How much would this bleed? Would it bleed like me . . . like last night . . . ? I could use your skull to drink from . . . open you up like a carcass and climb inside you . . . thrash about in your weak, wet chest . . . roast your heart with my breath and eat it whole. You think I'm weak? Because I wanted you inside me? It's just biology – just chemicals – you think I want to run away with you and carry your brats in my body . . . feed your spawn with my blood . . . you've got another thing coming Mister . . . come on! You think I want your child? You think I want to take your name? Look at me . . . what *is* your name? Your surname? I've never heard it . . . maybe you haven't got one? I'd be Mrs Scum, Mrs Barrow Boy . . . mmm? Is that what you want? A nice little wife? A nice girl like me? You dog who wears my crest upon your buttons. That's what you are! Buttons. You think I'd share you with my cook? *Come on* . . . aren't you having fun ?

She removes her hand and sits at the table.

Daddy will be home soon, he finds his desk open, second drawer down, his money gone. He rings on the bell – twice for his lackey – that's *you* – and then he sends for the police. And I say it was HIM officer. (*Cockney*.) 'He's the one what did it'. And I tell them everything. And then Daddy has a heart attack and drops down dead. End of the line. The train will terminate at this station. The bloodline clots. No heirs. No more of us. Dead. But what of the lackey? Oh, that'll be the pauper's line, third stop after the gutter, it ends in jail.

Enter **Christine**. *She stands in the doorway.*

And here's the mother. 'Got a fag, ducks?'

Christine *surveys the scene: the suitcase, the dead bird, the cash, the dress, the blood on* **John**'s face.

She produces a cut-throat razor from her bag.

Christine (*measured*)   I remembered at the gate; your razor's broke. You couldn't shave. You can now. I borrowed this from the gatekeeper.

*She hands **John** the razor.*

Christine   Go and shave. We're late for church.

John *exits.*

Julie   Christine, you're my friend, we've always had our little chats, haven't we? Listen –

Christine   Where were you going?

Julie   New York. Not my idea, but if you listen . . . oh you're angry . . . listen: me and John . . . we're in love with each other –

Christine   I don't want to know.

Julie   You see we simply can't stay here and –

Christine   He's not going anywhere.

Julie (*snaps*)   Please try to be calm, Christine!

Beat.

It's a very nice name, Christine. So we can't stay here for various reasons too complicated to go into but I've had this brilliant idea which is that all three of us go to New York together and we open a nightclub . . . I've got some money, you see . . . you mustn't tell anyone I stole it . . . and me and John would run it and you could be in charge of the kitchen. Wouldn't that be nice? Do say yes because if you say yes then everything'll be nice and not dreadful. Oh, can I have one?

Christine *gives **Miss Julie** a cigarette and a light.*

Julie   Thank you. You'd love New York . . . The Metropolitan . . . that's a museum and The Empire State Building which is so high that when you're at the top the people on the street look like insects . . . you're not allowed to drop a coin on them because it kills them . . . and in the winter the children skate on the lake in Central Park, when I was there with my father I skated . . . he made me . . .

She pauses, remembering something.

And I'm sure the nightclub will be a terrific success and there'll be dancing and we'll drink whenever we want because we'll own all the drink . . . and with your looks, I'm not flattering or patronising you, you'll meet a nice husband, a rich American, you'll see . . . the Americans are charmed by us . . . they die for the accent . . . and we'll live on the Upper . . . East Side . . . or West Side . . . East or West . . . it doesn't matter really . . . or we can always come home again . . . back here . . . or somewhere else . . . don't you think?

Christine   You believe all this?

Julie   No.

John *appears, the razor in his hand.*

Christine   So you were going to run away. You're as mad as she is.

He hands her the razor.

John   Show some respect, she's still your mistress.

Christine   What *this*?!

*She points at **Miss Julie**.*

This puddle! This is what comes of moral weakness.

She puts the razor down.

John   And you're superior? She slept with me, so did you, where's the difference?

Christine   Listen to him, cock of the walk! I've never sunk as low as her. Or you. I'm not a thief.

John   You stupid bitch! The whole war you traded on the black market, what's that, good honest toil?

Christine   I'm going to church.

John   That's right, you cling to your superstition.

Christine   Our saviour suffered and died on the cross for all our sins and if we approach him in faith and with a penitent heart, he will take all our sins upon him.

John   Including backhanders to the butcher?

Christine *picks up the wad of notes and puts them in her bag. Then she takes the car keys from the cupboard.*

Christine   And I'll take these in case anyone was thinking of leaving before his Lordship gets home.

She exits. Silence.

John   Christ, I despise religion.

Julie   So why practise it? Class is your religion.

Miss Julie *toys with the razor.* **John** *takes it from her.*

John   Don't do that, you'll hurt yourself.

Julie   I want to.

John   No you don't.

Julie   I do but I can't. Just like my father – he should've done it. The coward.

John   You're tired.

Julie   Shattered.

John   You want some tea?

Julie   No thanks.

John   I'm having some . . .

Julie   No.

He puts the kettle on. She picks up the razor again.

She didn't leave any cigarettes did she?

John   What do you think?

Pause.

Your father's not a coward.

Julie   Oh, he is.

She toys with the razor.

You don't know him. You don't know what it's like to be Daddy's special girl. Of course I love him, I love him as much as I hate him. He's inside my head all the time. And my mother. Who's to blame for what we are? It's a horrible, ugly mess. My thoughts are his, my feelings are hers. An endless circle.

John   Circles are always endless.

The bell rings. Three sharp rings, loud.

Your father's back!

He rushes to the phone, instinctively straightening his tie.

John (*in phone*)   This is John, sir . . . Yes, sir . . . Yes, sir . . . Yes, sir.

Julie   Three bags full, sir.

John   Very good, sir . . . excellent party, sir . . . no, not too much drinking, sir . . . thank you, sir . . . yes, everyone had an excellent time, sir. No, no damage, sir . . . Yes, right away.

He puts the phone down.

(*Panicking.*) He wants his shoes and his coffee immediately!

He looks for the shoes on the table. Gone. Then, horrified, he remembers he's wearing them. He pulls them off and puts them on the table.

Give these a once over will you? (*He stops, suddenly.*) Sorry.

Julie   You thought I was her?

John (*exiting*)   Yes, forgive me.

Julie (*to herself*)   It was nice.

She sits alone, holding the razor.

Presently, **John** *returns wearing his own shoes. He runs around, preparing: he fetches a coffee pot, china crockery and a silver tray. He polishes a teaspoon and then starts grinding coffee beans.*

Miss Julie *watches him, appalled at his servitude.*

Julie   Look at you . . . grinding away . . . so loyal . . . John The Baptist. And daddy is . . . Herod. And I am Salome.

John   You're still drunk.

She approaches him with the razor, suddenly holds it to his throat. He remains still.

Julie   I am Salome and you can have your revenge, John. Give the order. You know I can take orders. What does killing feel like, tell me how it feels.

She strokes his cheek with the razor.

John   It feels like nothing. You obey the order.

Julie   Give the order, Officer.

John   I'm not an Officer.

He grips her wrist to prevent her slashing him or herself. They move together slowly. A strange dance.

Julie   I know, it's not fair, is it? Give the order – deserter – boy – peasant. Order me.

Beat.

What would you do if Daddy rang his bell and ordered you to cut your throat? You'd obey, wouldn't you . . . because you must . . . because you were born to obey. Give the order, slave.

John   Do it yourself.

Julie   No fun on my own. Order me. Be the hypnotist at the village fair. You remember the fair. I saw you there that last summer, before the war . . . remember?

He nods.

You saw me . . . that's when I knew you wanted me, you were chained to Christine . . . already buried alive . . . but I know you saw me . . . you were hypnotised . . . describe my dress.

John   White with a pink ribbon . . .

Julie   Here . . .

She gestures across her throat with the razor. He gently takes it from her.

And you looked at me as we queued for the hypnotist, you looked at me with longing, you looked at the one who had everything and you stepped aside, you said, 'After you, Miss Julie'.

John   You smiled, you said:

Julie   Thank you, John.

John   How did you know my name?

Julie   Because I asked my father.

John   Why?

Julie   Because I wanted you. Because I'd felt your eyes upon me forever . . . because you do my father's dirty work . . . because you've always been watching me, waiting for me . . . because you want revenge . . . my father's angel with your eyes upon me forever.

Pause.

And the hypnotist says to his subject . . . 'Take this broom' and you feel that there's a broom in your hand and you take the broom and he says 'Sweep' and you sweep and afterwards you remember nothing.

John   You have to be asleep first.

Julie   I am asleep. The room is filled with smoke and you're an iron stove, you're a man dressed in black with a top hat, your eyes glow like coals when the fire dies and your face is white as ash.

He eases the razor into her hand.

John   Here's your broom . . .

Julie   Where do I go?

John   To the barn.

He whispers in her ear.

She turns to him, holding the razor, she nods.

They kiss briefly, tenderly.

As they slowly part the bell rings, once, loud.

He starts, she holds him.

Julie   It's only a bell. Pray for me . . .

John   I don't believe in God.

Julie   But pray for me.

The bell rings again, twice.

It's just a bell, my darling angel . . .

John   It's not just a bell. There's someone behind it. And a hand that sets it in motion . . . and a vast spinning universe that sets the hand in motion. And if you stop your ears it rings louder until you answer, until the police come . . . it's hell . . . and there's nothing else . . . *go.*

Miss Julie *walks to the door, the razor in her hand, she doesn't look back.*

She exits.

John *sits at the table.*

He starts to polish the shoes.

Twenty seconds.

Blackout.

Closer

For Debra

Closer was first presented in the Cottesloe auditorium of the Royal National Theatre, London, on 22 May 1997. The cast was as follows:

Alice	Liza Walker
Dan	Clive Owen
Larry	Ciaran Hinds
Anna	Sally Dexter

Closer transferred to the Lyttleton auditorium of the Royal National Theatre, London, on 16 October 1997. The cast was as follows:

Alice	Liza Walker
Dan	Mark Strong
Larry	Neil Dudgeon
Anna	Sally Dexter

Closer transferred to the Lyric Theatre in the West End, where it was presented by Robert Fox, on 19 March 1998. The cast was as follows:

Alice	Liza Walker
Dan	Lloyd Owen
Larry	Neil Pearson
Anna	Frances Barber

Director Patrick Marber
Designer Vicki Mortimer
Lighting Hugh Vanstone
Music Paddy Cunneen
Sound Simon Baker
Internet John Owens

Characters

Alice, *a girl from the town.*
Dan, *a man from the suburbs.*
Larry, *a man from the city.*
Anna, *a woman from the country.*

Setting
The play is set in London.

Scene One: January
Scene Two: June (the following year)
Scene Three: January (the following year)
Scene Four: January (the next day)
Scene Five: June (five months later)
Scene Six: June (a year later)
Scene Seven: September (three months later)
Scene Eight: October (a month later)
Scene Nine: November (a month later)
Scene Ten: December (a month later)
Scene Eleven: January (a month later)
Scene Twelve: July (six months later)

The above dates are for information only. They should not be included in any production programme or design.

All settings should be minimal.

Note
This revised version of *Closer* replaces those previously published and is the sole authorised version of the play.

An alternative 'spoken' version of Act One, Scene Three appears at the end of this text.

Act One

Scene One

Hospital.

Early morning. (January.)

Alice *is sitting. She is wearing a black coat. She has a rucksack by her side. Also, an old, brown, leather briefcase.*

She rolls down one sock. She has a cut on her leg, quite bloody. She looks at it. She picks some strands of wool from the wound.

She looks at the briefcase. Thinks. Looks around. Opens it. She searches inside. She pulls out some sandwiches in silver foil. She looks at the contents, smiles, puts them back in the briefcase. Then she removes a green apple from the briefcase. She shines the apple and bites into it.

As she starts to chew **Dan** *enters. He wears a suit and an overcoat. He stops, watches her eating his apple. He is holding two hot drinks in styrofoam cups. After a while she sees him and smiles.*

Alice   Sorry. I was looking for a cigarette.

Dan   I've given up.

He hands her a drink.

Alice   Thanks.

He checks his watch.

Have you got to be somewhere?

Dan   Work.

They sip their drinks.

Didn't fancy my sandwiches?

Alice   I don't eat fish.

Dan   Why not?

Alice   Fish piss in the sea.

Dan   So do children.

Alice   I don't eat children either. What's your work?

Dan   I'm a . . . sort of journalist.

Alice   What *sort*?

Beat.

Dan   I write obituaries.

Beat.

Alice   Do you like it . . . in the *dying* business?

Dan   It's a living.

Alice   Did you grow up in a graveyard?

Dan   Yeah. Suburbia.

Beat.

Alice   Do you think a doctor will come?

Dan   Eventually. Does it hurt?

Alice   I'll live.

Dan   Shall I put your leg up?

Alice   *Why?*

Dan   That's what people do in these situations.

Alice   What is this 'situation'?

They look at each other.

Dan   Do you *want* me to put your leg up?

Alice   Yes, please.

Dan *lifts her leg on to a chair, offers his mobile phone.*

Dan   Is there anyone you'd like to phone?

Alice   I don't know anyone.
Who cut off your crusts?

Dan   Me.

Alice   Did your mother cut off your crusts when you were
a little boy?

Dan   I believe she did, yes.

Alice   You should eat your crusts.

Dan   You should stop smoking.

Beat.

Alice   Thank you for scraping me off the road.

Dan   My pleasure.

Alice   You *knight.*

Dan *looks at her.*

Dan   You *damsel.*
Why didn't you look?

Alice   I never look where I'm going.

Dan   We stood at the lights, I looked into your eyes and
then you . . . stepped into the road.

Alice   Then what?

Dan   You were lying on the ground, you focused on me,
you said, 'Hallo, stranger.'

Alice   What a slut.

Dan   I noticed your leg was cut.

Alice   Did you notice my *legs?*

Dan   Quite possibly.

Alice   Then what?

Dan   The cabbie got out. He crossed himself. He said,
'Thank fuck, I thought I'd killed her.' I said, 'Let's get her to

a hospital.' He hesitated . . . (I think he thought there'd be paperwork and he'd be held 'responsible'), so I said, with a slight sneer, 'Please, just drop us at the hospital.'

Alice   Show me the sneer.

Dan *considers then sneers.*

Alice   Very good. *Buster.*

Dan   We put you in the cab and came here.

Alice   What was I doing?

Dan   You were murmuring, 'I'm very sorry for all the inconvenience.' I had my arm round you . . . your head was on my shoulder.

Alice   Was my head . . . *lolling?*

Dan   That's exactly what it was doing.

Pause.

Alice   You'll be late for work.

Dan   Are you saying you want me to go?

Alice   I'm saying you'll be late for work.

Beat.

Dan   Why were you at Blackfriars Bridge?

Alice   I'd been to a club near the meat market . . . *Smithfield.* Do you go clubbing?

Dan   No, I'm too old.

Alice   How old?

Dan   Thirty-five.

Alice   Half-time?

Dan   Thank you very much. So, you were *clubbing* . . .

Alice   Then I went for a walk, I went to see the meat being unloaded.

Dan   The carcasses, why?

Alice   Because they're repulsive.
Then I found this tiny park . . . it's a graveyard too.
Postman's Park. Do you know it?

Dan   No.

Alice   There's a memorial to ordinary people who died
saving the lives of others. It's most *curious.*
Then I decided to go to Borough – so I went to Blackfriars
Bridge to cross the river.

Dan   That *park* . . . it's near here?

Alice   Yes.

Dan   Is there a . . . statue?

Alice   A Minotaur.

Dan   I <u>do</u> know it. We sat there . . . (my mother's dead)
. . . my father and I sat there the afternoon she died.

She died *here*, actually. <u>She</u> was a smoker.

(*Remembering.*) My father . . . ate . . . an egg sandwich . . . his
hands shook with grief . . . pieces of egg fell on the grass . . .
butter on his top lip.

But I don't remember a memorial.

Alice   Is your father still alive?

Dan   Clinging on. He's in a home.

Alice   How did you end up writing obituaries? What did
you *really* want to be?

Dan (*smiles*)   Oh . . . I had dreams of being a writer but I
had no voice.
What am I saying? I had no *talent.*
So . . . I ended up in the 'Siberia' of journalism.

Alice   Tell me what you do, I want to imagine you in
Siberia.

Dan   Really?

Alice   Yes.

Beat.

Dan   Well . . . we call it 'the obits page'. There's three of us; me, Harry and *Graham*. When I get to work, without fail, Graham will say, 'Who's on the slab?' Meaning, did anyone important die overnight – are you *sure* you want to know?

Alice   Yes.

Dan   Well, if someone 'important' did die we go to the 'deep freeze' which is a computer containing all the obituaries and we'll find the dead person's life.

Alice   People's obituaries are written when they're still alive?

Dan   Some people's.
If no one important has died then *Harry* – he's the editor – he decides who we lead with and we check facts, make calls, polish the prose.
Some days I might be asked to deal with the widows or widowers; they try to persuade us to run an obituary of their husbands or wives. They feel we're dishonouring their loved ones if we don't but . . . most of them are . . . well, there isn't the space.
At six, we stand round the computer and read the next day's page, make final changes, put in a few euphemisms to amuse ourselves . . .

Alice   Such as?

Dan   'He was a convivial fellow', meaning he was an alcoholic.
'He valued his privacy' – gay.
'He *enjoyed* his privacy' . . . raging queen.

Pause. **Alice** *slowly strokes* **Dan**'*s face. He is unnerved but not unwilling.*

Alice   And what would your euphemism be?

Dan (*softly*)   For me?

Alice   Mmm.

Dan   He was . . . *reserved*.

Alice   And mine?

Dan   She was . . . *disarming*.

Beat.

Alice   How did you get this job?

Dan   They ask you to write your own obituary: if it amuses, you're in.

They are close. Looking at each other.
Larry *walks past in a white coat.* **Dan** *stops him.*

Dan   Excuse me, we've been waiting quite a long time . . .

Larry   I'm sorry, it's not my . . .

He is about to walk away. He glances briefly at **Alice***. 'Pretty girl.' He stops.*

What happened?

Alice   I was hit by a cab.

Dan   She was unconscious for about ten seconds.

Larry   May I?

He looks at the wound and examines her leg with interest.

You can feel your toes?

Alice   Yes.

Larry   What's this?

Larry *traces the line of a scar on her leg.*

Alice   It's a scar.

Larry   Yes, I know it's a *scar*. How did you get it?

Alice   In America. A truck.

Larry *looks at the scar.*

Larry   Awful job.

Alice   I was in the middle of nowhere.

Larry   You'll be fine.

Larry *makes to leave.*

Alice   Can I have one?

Larry *looks at her, she nods at his pocket.*

Alice   A cigarette.

Larry *takes out his pack of cigarettes and removes one.*
Alice *reaches for it, he withdraws it.*

Larry   Don't smoke it here.

He hands her the cigarette.

Dan   Thank you.

Larry *exits.* **Alice** *lights the cigarette.*

Alice   Want a drag?

Dan   Yes but no. What were you doing, in 'the middle of nowhere'?

Alice   Travelling.

Beat.

Dan   Alone?

Alice   With . . . a *male*.

Beat.

Dan   What happened to this male?

Alice   I don't know, I ran away.

Dan   Where?

Alice   New York.

Dan   Just like that?

Alice   It's the only way to leave; 'I don't love you any more, goodbye.'

Dan   Supposing you do still love them?

Alice   You don't leave.

Dan   You've never left someone you still love?

Alice   No.

Beat.

Dan   When did you come back?

Alice   Yesterday.

Dan   Where are your belongings?

Alice *points to her rucksack.*

Alice   I'm a waif.

Beat.

Dan   Did you like New York?

Alice   Sure.

Dan   Were you . . . studying?

Alice   *Stripping.*

She looks at him.

Look at your little eyes.

Dan   I can't see my little eyes.

Alice   They're popping out. You're a cartoon.

Beat.

Dan   Were you . . . 'good' at it?

Alice   *Exceptional.*

Dan   Why?

Alice   I know what men want.

Dan   Really?

Alice   Oh yes.

Dan   Tell me . . .

Alice considers.

Alice   Men want a girl who looks like a boy.
They want to protect her but she must be a survivor.
And she must <u>come</u> . . . like a *train* . . . but with . . . *elegance*.

What do *you* want?

Pause.

Dan   Who was this . . . *male?*

Alice   A customer. But once I was his he hated me
stripping.

Dan *smiles.*

Dan   What do *you* want?

Alice   To be loved.

Dan   That simple?

Alice   It's a big want.

She looks at him.

Do you have a girlfriend?

Dan   Yeah, *Ruth* . . . she's called Ruth. She's a linguist.

He looks at **Alice**.

Will you meet me after work?

Alice   No, take the day off. Don't go and see '*who's on the
slab*'. I'll call in for you and say you're sick.

Dan   I *can't.*

Alice   Don't be such a pussy.

Dan   I might be anyone, I might be a psychotic.

Alice   I've met psychotics, you're <u>not</u>. *Phone.*

She holds out her hand, **Dan** *gives her his mobile.*

Dan   Memory One.

Alice *punches in the number.*

Alice   Who do I speak to?

Dan   Harry Masters.

Alice   What's your name?

Dan   Mr Daniel Woolf. What's *your* name?

Beat.

Alice   Alice. My name is Alice Ayres.

Blackout.

Scene Two

Anna's *studio.*

Late afternoon. June (the following year).

Anna *stands behind her camera.* **Dan** *sits.* **Anna** *takes a shot.*

Anna   Good.

Shot.

Don't move.

Shots.

Dan   What was this building?

Anna   A refuge for fallen women.

Shot.

Dan   Wasn't there a river here?

Anna   *The Fleet*. They built over it in the eighteenth century.

Dan   A buried river.

Shot.

Anna   If you stand on Blackfriars Bridge you can see where it comes out.

Dan   I think I will.

Anna   You must.

Shot.

Stay there.

Shots.

It inspired an 'urban legend' – a bit like the alligators in New York. People thought that pigs were breeding underground and then one day this big, fat boar swam out into the Thames and trotted off along the Embankment.

Dan   So it was true?

Anna   No, it escaped. From *Smithfield*.

Dan   Pigs can swim?

Anna   Surprisingly well.

Shots.

Relax.

Anna *changes film, adjusts a light, etc.*
Dan *stands up.*

Dan   Do you mind if I smoke?

Anna   If you must.

Dan   I don't have to.

Anna   Then don't.

She looks at **Dan**.

I liked your book.

Dan Thanks . . .

Anna When's it published?

Dan Next year, how come you read it?

Anna Your publisher sent me a manuscript, I read it last night. You kept me up till *four*.

Dan I'm flattered.

Anna Is your anonymous heroine based on someone real?

Beat.

Dan She's . . . someone called Alice.

Anna How does she feel about you stealing her life?

Dan *Borrowing* her life. I'm dedicating the book to her, she's pleased.

He is staring at her, **Anna** *turns, looks at him.*

Pause.

Do you exhibit?

Anna Next summer.

Dan Portraits?

Anna Yes.

Dan Of who?

Beat.

Anna Strangers.

Anna *gestures for him to sit again.*
She checks the light on him with a meter.

Dan How do your strangers feel about *you* stealing *their* lives?

Anna *Borrowing.*

Anna *adjusts his hair.*

Dan   Am I a stranger?

Anna   No . . . you're a job.

Pause.

Dan   You're beautiful.

Beat.

Anna   No I'm not.

Anna *looks down the lens.*

Chin up, you're a sloucher.

Shots.

Dan   You didn't find it obscene?

Anna   What?

Dan   The book.

Anna   No, I thought it was . . . *accurate.*

Shot.

Dan   About what?

Anna   About sex. About love.

Shot.

Dan   In what way?

Anna   You *wrote* it.

Dan   But you *read* it. Till *four*.

Dan *looks at her,* **Anna** *looks down the lens.*

Anna   Don't raise your eyebrows, you look smug.

Shot.

Stand up.

Dan *stands up.*

Dan   But you did *like* it?

Anna   Yes, but I could go off it.

Shots.

Dan   Any criticisms?

Anna *considers.*

Anna   Bad title.

Dan   Got a better one?

Anna   Really?

Dan   Yeh . . .

Beat.

Anna   'The Aquarium'.

They look at each other.

Beat.

Dan   You liked the dirty bit . . . ?

Anna   Some of it.

Dan   You like aquariums?

Anna   Fish are therapeutic.

Dan   Hang out in aquariums, do you?

Anna   When I can.

Dan   Good for picking up 'Strangers'?

Anna   *Photographing* strangers. I took my first picture in the one at London Zoo.

Silence.

Dan (*gently*)   Come here . . .

Pause.

Anna *moves towards him, slowly. She stops.*

Anna   I don't kiss strange men.

Dan   Neither do I.

They kiss. Ten seconds. **Anna** *slowly pulls back.*

Anna   Do you and this . . . *Alice* . . . live together?

Dan *considers.*

Dan   . . . Yes . . .

Anna (*nods*)   'She has one address in her address book; ours . . . under "H" for home.'

Dan *touches her face.*

Dan   I've cut that line.

Anna   Why?

Dan   Too sentimental.

Anna *gently takes his hand from her face, looks at it and then pulls away from him.*

Dan   Are you married?

Anna   Yes.

Dan *turns away, she looks at him.*

Anna   No.

Dan *turns back.*

Anna   *Yes.*

Dan   <u>Which</u>?

Anna   Separated.

Dan   Do you have any children?

Anna   No.

Dan   Would you like some?

Anna   Yes, but not today.

She shuts her camera case and begins to pack up, session over.

Would *Alice* like children?

Dan   She's too young.

He glances at his watch.

Actually . . . she's coming to meet me here . . . quite soon.

Anna   Why are you wasting her time?

Dan   I'm not. I'm grateful to her . . . she's . . . completely loveable and completely unleaveable.

Anna   And you don't want someone else to get their dirty hands on her?

Beat.

Dan   Maybe.

Anna   Men are crap.

Dan   But all the same . . .

Anna   They're still crap.

The door buzzer goes.

Your muse.

Dan *looks at* **Anna**.

Dan (*ironic*)   You've ruined my life.

Anna   You'll get over it.

They look at each other. **Dan** *goes to exit.*

Dan . . .

Dan *turns.*

Anna   Your shirt.

Dan *exits tucking his shirt into his trousers.*

Silence.

Anna *thinks*.

Dan *enters with* **Alice**. *Her hair is a different colour to Scene One*.

Dan   Anna . . . Alice.

Anna   Hi.

Alice *looks at* **Anna**.

Alice   I'm sorry if you're still working.

Anna   No, we've just finished.

Alice   Was he well-behaved?

Anna   Reasonably.

Alice   Is he photogenic?

Anna   I think so.

Alice   Did you steal his soul?

Anna   Would you like some tea?

Alice   No thanks, I've been serving it all day. Can I use the . . . ?

Anna (*gestures*)   Through there.

Alice *exits*.

Anna   *She* is beautiful.

Dan   Yes, she is.

He looks at **Anna**.

I've got to see you.

Anna   No!

Dan   Why are you getting all . . . 'sisterly'?

Anna   I'm not getting 'sisterly', I don't want trouble.

Dan   I'm not trouble.

Anna   You're taken.

Pause.

Dan   I've *got* to see you.

Anna (*shakes her head*)   <u>Tough</u>.

Pause. **Alice** *enters.*

Alice   I'm a block of ice.

Dan *goes to* **Alice** *and rubs her.*

Alice (*to* **Anna**)   Will you take *my* photo?
I've never been photographed by a professional before.
I'd really appreciate it, I can pay you.

Pause.

Anna   No . . . I'd like to . . .

Alice (*to* **Dan**)   Only if *you* don't mind.

Dan   Why should I?

Alice   Because you'll have to go away.
(*To* **Anna**.) We don't want *him* here while we're working, do we?

Anna   No, we don't.

Beat.

Dan   . . . *Right* . . . I'll wait in the pub on the corner . . .

He kisses **Alice**.

Have fun.

(*To* **Anna**.) Thank you. Good luck with your exhibition.

Anna   Good luck with your book.

Dan   Thanks.

Dan *exits, lighting a cigarette as he goes.*

Alice   You've got an exhibition?

Anna   Only a small one. Take a seat.

Alice *sits.*
Anna *busies herself with the camera, checks lights, etc.*
Alice *watches her.*

Anna   I read Dan's book, you've had . . . quite a life.

Alice   Thanks.

Are you single?

Anna   . . . Yes.

Alice   Who was your last boyfriend?

Anna *is unsure where this is leading.*

Anna   My husband . . .

Alice   What happened to him?

Beat.

Anna   Someone younger.

Alice   What did he do?

Anna   He made money. In the City.

Alice   We used to get those in the clubs. *Wall Street boys.*

Anna   So . . . these places were quite . . . upmarket?

Alice   Some of them, but I preferred the dives.

Anna   Why?

Alice   The poor are more generous.

Anna *looks into the camera.*

Anna   You've got a great face.

She focuses.

How do you feel about Dan using your life, for his book?

Alice   None of your fucking business.

She stares at **Anna**.

When he let me in . . . downstairs, he had . . . this . . . '*look*'.

I just listened to your . . . *conversation*.

Silence.

Anna   I don't know what to say.

Alice (*gently*)   Take my picture.

Pause.

Anna   I'm not a thief, Alice.

She looks down the lens.

Head up . . .

Alice *raises her head, she is in tears.*

Anna   You look beautiful. Turn to me . . .

She takes her shots. They look at each other.

Good.

Blackout.

Scene Three

Internet

Early evening. January (the following year).

Dan *is in his flat sitting at a table with a computer. There is a Newton's Cradle on the table. Writerly sloth, etc.*

Larry *is sitting at his hospital desk with a computer. He is wearing a white coat.*

They are in separate rooms.

The scene is silent. Their 'dialogue' appears on a large screen simultaneous to their typing it.

Dan   Hallo.

Larry   hi

Larry   How RU?

Larry   ok

Dan   Cum here often?

Larry   1st time.

Dan   A Virgin. Welcome. What's your name?

Larry   Larry. U?

Dan *considers.*

Dan   Anna

Larry   Nice 2 meet U

Dan   I love COCK

Pause.

Larry   Youre v.forward

Dan   And UR chatting on 'LONDON FUCK'. Do U want sex?

Larry   yes. describe u.

Dan   Dark hair. Dirty mouth. Epic Tits.

Larry   define epic

Dan   36DD

Larry   Nice arse?

Dan   Y

Larry   Becos i want 2 know

Dan *smiles.*

Dan   No, 'Y' means 'Yes'.

Larry   O

Dan   I want 2 suck U senseless.

Larry   B my guest

Dan   Sit on my face Fuckboy.

Larry   I'm there

Dan   Wear my wet knickers.

Beat.

Larry   ok

Dan   RU well hung?

Larry   9£

Larry (*speaking*)   Shit.

Larry (*typing*)   9″

Dan   GET IT OUT

Larry *considers and then unzips. He puts his hand in his trousers. The phone on his desk rings. Loud. He jumps.*

Larry (*speaking*)   Wait.

Larry (*typing*)   wait

Larry *picks up the phone.* **Dan** *lights a cigarette.*

Larry (*speaking*)   <u>Yes</u>. What's the histology? *Progressive?* Sounds like an atrophy.

Larry *puts the phone down and goes back to his keyboard.* **Dan** *clicks the balls on his Newton's Cradle.*

Larry   hallo?

Dan *looks at his screen.*

Larry   anna

Larry (*speaking*)   Bollocks.

Larry (*typing*)   ANNA? WHERE RU?

Dan   Hey, big Larry, what d'you wank about?

Larry *considers.*

Larry   Ex-girlfriends.

Dan   Not current g-friends?

Larry   Never

Dan *smiles.*

Dan   Tell me your sex-ex fantasy . . .

Larry   Hotel room . . . they tie me up . . . tease me . . . won't let me come. They fight over me, 6 tonges on my cock, ballls, perineum etc.

Dan   All hail the Sultan of Twat?

Larry *laughs.*

Larry   Anna, wot do U wank about?

Dan *thinks.*

Dan   Strangers.

Larry   details . . .

Dan   They form a Q and I attend to them like a cum hungry bitch,1 in each hole and both hands.

Larry   then?

Dan   They cum in my mouth arse tits cunt hair.

Larry (*speaking*)   Jesus.

Larry*'s phone rings. He picks up the receiver and replaces it without answering. Then he takes it off the hook.*

Larry (*typing*)   then?

Dan   i lik it off like the dirty slut I am. Wait,have to type with 1 hand . . . I'm cumming right now . . . ohohohohohohohohohohohohohohohohohohohooooooooo oooooooooooooooooooooooooooooooooooooooooooooo +_)(*&^%$£"!_*)&%^&!"!"£$%%^^%&^%&&*&*((*(*)&^ %*((£££

Pause. **Larry***, motionless, stares at his screen.*

Larry   was it good?

Dan   No.

Larry *shakes his head.*

Larry   I'm shocked

Dan   PARADISE SHOULD BE SHOCKING

Larry   RU4 real?

Beat.

Dan   MEET ME

Pause.

Larry   serious?

Dan   Y

Larry   when

Dan   NOW

Larry   can't. I'm a Dr. Must do rounds.

Dan *smiles.* **Larry** *flicks through his desk diary.*

Dan   Don't b a pussy. Life without riskisdeath. Desire,like the world,is am accident. The bestsex is anon. We liv as we dream,ALONE. I'll make u cum like a train.

Larry   Tomorrow,1 pm,where?

Dan *thinks.*

Dan   The Aquarium, London Zoo & then HOTEL.

Larry   How will U know me?

Dan   Bring white coat

Larry   ?

Dan   Dr + Coat = Horn 4 me

Larry   !

Dan   I send U a rose my love . . .

Larry   ?

Dan   (@)
       |
      \ |
       | /
       |
       |

Larry   Thanks. CU at Aquarium. Bye Anna.

Dan   Bye Larry xxxxx

Larry   xxxxxx

They look at their screens.

Blackout.

Scene Four

Aquarium.

Afternoon. January (the next day).

Anna *is sitting on a bench, alone. She has a camera. She looks at the fish, occasionally referring to her guide book.*

Larry *enters.*
He sees **Anna**. *He checks her out and smiles.*
Anna *sees him and vaguely nods, acknowledging his presence.*

Larry   Anna?

Anna   . . . Yes . . . ?

Larry *unbuttons his overcoat and holds it open. He is wearing his white coat underneath.*

Larry   I've got 'The Coat'.

Anna *observes him.*

Anna   Yes, you *have*.

Larry   'The White Coat.'

Anna   So I see . . .

Larry   I'm Larry. (*Dirty.*) 'The Doctor.'

Beat.

Anna   Hallo, Doctor Larry.

Larry   Feel free to call me . . . '*The Sultan*'.

Anna   *Why?*

Larry (*laughs*)   I can't believe these things actually *happen*. I thought . . . if you turned up, you'd be a bit of a trout . . . but you're bloody gorgeous.

Anna   Thanks.

Beat.

Larry   You mentioned a hotel . . .

Anna *looks at him, trying to work out who he is.*

Larry   No rush.

He checks his watch.

Actually, there *is*, I've got to be in surgery by three.

Anna   Are you having an operation?

Larry (*laughs*)   No, I'm *doing* one.

Anna   You really *are* a doctor?

Larry   I said I was. (*Sudden panic.*) You are . . . <u>*Anna*</u>?

Anna   Yes. I'm sorry, have we met somewhere?

Larry   Don't play games, you . . . 'Nymph of the Net'. (*Confused.*) You were filthy *yesterday*.

Anna   Was I?

Larry   YES. 'Wear my wet knickers', 'Sit on my face', 'I'm a cum hungry bitch typing with one . . .'

Anna *smiles*.

Larry   Why do I feel like a pervert?

Anna   I think . . . you're the victim . . . of a medic's prank.

Pause.

Larry   I am *so* sorry.

Larry *exits*. **Anna** *chuckles*. **Larry** *re-enters*.

Larry   NO. We spoke on the Net but now you've *seen* me you don't . . . it's *fine*, I'm not going to get <u>upset</u> about it.

Anna   Then why are you upset?

Larry   I'm not, I'm <u>frustrated</u>.

Anna   I don't even have a computer, I'm a photographer.

Larry *considers*.

Larry   Where were *you* between the hours of 5.45 and 6.00 p.m., yesterday?

Anna   I was in a café seeing . . . an acquaintance.

Larry   Name?

Anna   Alice Ayres.

Larry   The nature of your business?

Anna (*amused*)   Photographic business. Where were *you* between those hours?

Larry   On the Net talking to you.

Anna   No.

Larry   Well, I was talking to *someone*.

Anna (*realising*)   Pretending to *be* me.

You were talking to Daniel Woolf.

Larry   Who?

Anna   He's Alice's boyfriend. She told me yesterday that he plays around on the Net. It's _him_.

Larry   No, I was talking to a woman.

Anna   How do you know?

Larry   Because . . . believe me, she was a woman, I got a _huge_ . . . She was a <u>woman</u>.

Anna   No, she wasn't.

Larry   She wasn't, was she.

Anna   No.

Larry   What a CUNT. Sorry.

Anna   I'm a grown-up, 'Cunt Away'.

Larry   Thanks. This . . . '_bloke_' . . .

Anna   Daniel Woolf.

Larry   How do you know him?

Anna   I don't know him really, I took his photo for a book he wrote.

Larry   I hope it sank without trace.

Anna   It's on its way.

Larry   There is justice in the world. What's it called?

Anna (_smiles_)   'The Aquarium'.

Larry   What a PRICK. He's <u>advertising</u>!
Why? Why would he pretend to be you?

Anna   He likes me.

Larry   Funny way of showing it, can't he send you flowers?

He produces a crumpled rose from his coat pocket. He hands it to **Anna**.

Here.

Anna   . . . Thanks . . .

She looks at the rose, then at **Larry***.*

Wonderful thing, the Internet.

Larry   Oh yes.

Anna   The possibility of genuine global communication, the first great democratic medium.

Larry   Absolutely, it's the future.

Anna   Two boys tossing in cyberspace.

Larry   *He* was the tosser.

I'll say this for him, he can *write*.

He looks at **Anna***.*

Is he in love with you?

Anna   I don't know. No.

Larry   Are you in love with him?

Anna   I hardly know him, no.

Larry   But you're sort of . . . interested?

Anna   I think he's . . . *interesting*.

Beat.

Larry   So what are you doing here?

Pause.

Anna   Looking at fish.

Anna *looks away from him.*

Larry (*gently*)   Are you all right?

Anna *nods.*

Larry   You can tell me . . .

Anna   Because you're a doctor?

Larry   Because I'm *here*.

Anna *turns to him.*

Larry   Crying is allowed.

Anna   I'm not allowed. Thanks, anyway.

Larry   I'm famed for my bedside manner.

Anna *raises her camera,* **Larry** *covers his face.*

Larry   Don't, I look like a criminal in photos.

Anna   Please, it's my birthday.

Larry (*dropping his hands*)   Really?

Anna *takes his photo.*

Anna   Yes. (*Rueful.*) Really.

They look at each other.

Larry   Happy birthday.

Blackout.

Scene Five

Gallery.

Evening. June (five months later).

Alice *is looking at a huge photograph of herself. She has a bottle of lager. She wears a black dress.*

Dan *has a glass of wine. A slightly shabby black suit. He looks at* **Alice** *looking at the image.*

Dan   Cheers.

She turns. They drink. **Dan** *admires the photo.*

You're the belle of the bullshit. You look beautiful.

Alice   I'm *here*.

Dan *looks at* **Alice**, *smiles*.

Alice   A man came into the café today and said, 'Hey, *waitress*, what are you waiting for?'

Dan   Funny guy.

Alice   I said, 'I'm waiting for a man to come in here and *fuck me sideways* with a beautiful line like that.'

Dan (*smiles*)   What did he do?

Alice   He asked for a cup of tea with two sugars.

She looks at him.

I'm waiting for *you*.

Dan   To do what?

Beat.

Alice (*gently*)   Leave me.

Dan (*concerned*)   I'm not going to leave you. I totally love you. What is this?

Alice   Please let me come . . .

Dan *turns away.*

Alice   I want to *be there* for you. Are you ashamed of me?

Dan   Of course not. I've told you, I want to be alone.

Alice   Why?

Dan   To *grieve* . . . to think.

Alice   I love you, why won't you let me?

Dan   It's only a weekend.

Alice   Why won't you let me *love* you?

Silence.

We've never spent a weekend in the country.

Dan   Well . . . we will.

He turns, drinks. He looks offstage and smiles at something he sees.

Harry's here . . . pissed as a newt.

He wants me to go back to 'obits' . . . says they miss me.

Alice   Poor Harry, you know he's in love with you.

Dan   No he's not.

He glances offstage again.

Is he?

Alice (*smiles*)   <u>Yes</u>. Do you want to go back?

Dan   We're very poor . . .

Alice   What about your writing?

Dan *shrugs.*

Dan   Look . . . I'm going to say hallo and goodbye to Anna and then I'll get a cab to the station, OK?

Buster?

I love you.

He kisses her forehead.

Alice (*softly*)   Kiss my lips . . .

Dan   Sorry.

He kisses her on the lips.

I'll call you as soon as I get there.

Dan *exits as* **Larry** *enters. They almost collide.*
Larry *regards the departing* **Dan**.

Alice *lights a cigarette, she uses her bottle as an ashtray.*

Larry *is wearing a suit with a black cashmere sweater with a collar. He has a bottle of wine and a glass.*
Alice *looks at him, curious.*

Larry   Evening.

Alice   Are you a waiter?

Larry   No, I'm a refugee escaping from the glittering babble.

He looks at the photo and then at his exhibition price list.

And . . . *you* are . . . '*Young Woman, London*'.

He looks at **Alice**.

Pricey. Do you like it?

Alice   No.

Larry   Well, you should. What were you so sad about?

Alice   Life.

Larry   What's that then?

Alice *smiles*.

Larry (*gesturing to the photos*)   What d'you reckon, in general?

Alice   You want to talk about *art*?

Larry   I know it's *vulgar* to discuss 'The Work' at an opening of 'The Work' but *someone's* got to do it. Serious, what d'you think?

Alice   It's a lie.
It's a bunch of sad strangers photographed beautifully and all the rich <u>fuckers</u> who appreciate *art* say it's beautiful because that's what they <u>want</u> to see.
But the people in the photos are sad and alone but the pictures make the world *seem* beautiful.
So, the exhibition is <u>reassuring</u>, which makes it a lie, and everyone loves a <u>Big Fat Lie</u>.

Larry   I'm the Big Fat Liar's boyfriend.

Alice   Bastard!

Larry   Larry.

Alice   Alice.

Beat. **Alice** *moves in on him.*

So . . . you're Anna's boyfriend?

Larry   A princess can kiss a frog.

Alice   How long have you been seeing her?

Larry   Four months. We're in 'the first flush'.
It's <u>Paradise</u>. All my nasty habits amuse her . . .

He gazes at **Alice**.

You shouldn't smoke.

Alice   Fuck off.

Larry   I'm a doctor, I'm supposed to say things like that.

Alice *now realises where she's seen him before. She holds out her
packet of cigarettes.*

Alice   Want one?

Larry   <u>No</u>.

Alice *continues to offer the packet.*

Larry   *Yes.* No. Fuck it, <u>yes</u>. NO. I've given up.

He watches her smoking.

Pleasure and self-destruction, the perfect poison.

Alice *gives him a dirty smile.*

Larry   Anna told me your bloke wrote a book, any good?

Alice   Of course.

Larry   It's about *you*, isn't it?

Alice   Some of me.

Larry   Oh? What did he leave out?

Beat.

Alice   The truth.

Beat.

Larry   Is he here? Your *bloke*.

Alice   Yeah, he's talking to your *bird*.

Larry *glances offstage, thinks, then returns to* **Alice**.

Larry   *So* . . . you were a stripper?

Alice (*flirtatious*)   Yeah . . . *and*?

Larry *sees the scar on her leg.*

Larry   Mind if I ask how you got that?

Beat.

Alice   You've asked me this before.

Larry   When?

Alice   Two and a half years ago. I was in hospital. You looked at my leg.

Larry   How did you remember me?

Alice   It was a memorable day.
You didn't really want to stop but you did, you were off for a crafty smoke.
You gave me a cigarette.

Larry   Well, I don't smoke now and nor should you.

Alice   But you *used* to go and smoke. *On the sly.*

Larry   Yeah, in a little park near the hospital.

Alice   *Postman's Park?*

Larry   That's the one.

Alice *takes a swig from his bottle.*

Larry   And . . . the *scar*?

Alice   A mafia hit man broke my leg.

Larry (*disbelieving*)   Really?

Alice   Absolutely.

Larry   Doesn't look like a break . . .

Alice   What does it look like?

Larry   Like something went into it. (*Tentative.*) A knife, maybe . . .

Alice   When I was eight . . . some metal went into my leg when my parents' car crashed . . . when they *died*. Happy now?

Larry   Sorry, it was none of my business. I'm supposed to be off duty.

Alice *looks at him.*

Alice   Is it nice being good?

Larry   I'm not good.

He looks at her, close.

What about *you*?

He gently strokes her face, she lets him.

I'm seeing my first private patient tomorrow. Tell me I'm not a sell-out.

Alice   You're not a sell-out.

Larry   *Thanks.* You take care.

Alice   I will, you too.

Alice *exits.* **Larry** *watches her go.*
Larry *exits as* **Dan** *enters elsewhere.*
Dan *carries a small suitcase. He checks his watch and waits, nervously.*

Anna *enters.*

Pause. They look at each other.

Anna   I can't talk for long.

Dan   Bit of a do, isn't it?

Anna   Yeah, I hate it.

Dan   But you're *good* at it.

So, he's a *dermatologist*. Can you get more boring than that?

Anna   Obituarist?

Dan   Failed novelist, please.

Anna   I was sorry about your book.

Dan   Thanks, I blame the title.

Anna (*smiles*)   I blame the critics. You must write another one.

Dan   Why can't failure be attractive?

Anna   It's not a failure.

Dan   It's *perceived* to be, therefore it is. Pathetically, I needed praise. A *real* writer is . . . above such concerns.

Anna   Romantic tosh.

Dan   Ever had bad reviews? Well, shut up then.

Talk to *Doctor Larry* about photography, do you?

Is he a fan of Man Ray or Karsh?

He'll <u>bore</u> you.

Anna   No he won't – he <u>doesn't</u>, actually.

Dan (*exasperated*)   I cannot believe I made this happen.

What were you <u>doing</u> at the Aquarium?

(*Joking.*) Thinking of me?

Anna   No. How's Alice?

Dan   She's fine. Do you love him?

Anna   Yes, very much.

Beat.

Dan (*alarmed*)   You're not going to *marry* him?

Anna   I might.

Dan   *Don't*. Marry me. Children, everything.
You don't want <u>his</u> children – three little stooges in white coats.
Don't marry him, marry me.
Grow old with me . . . *die* with me . . . wear a battered cardigan on the beach in Bournemouth.
<u>*Marry me*</u>.

Anna (*smiles*)   I don't *know* you.

Dan   <u>Yes you do</u>.
I couldn't feel what I feel for you unless you felt it too.
Anna, *we're in love* – it's not our fault, stop wasting his time.

Anna   I haven't *seen* you for a <u>year</u>.

Dan   Yes <u>you have</u>.

Anna   Only because you *stalked* me outside my studio.

Dan   I didn't <u>stalk</u> . . . I . . . *lurked*.
And when I wasn't there you looked for me.

Anna   How do you know, if you weren't *there*?

Dan   Because I <u>was</u> there . . . lurking from a distance.
(I love your work, by the way, it's tragic).

Anna (*sarcastic*)   Thanks.

Dan *gestures to his suitcase.*

Dan   I know this isn't 'appropriate,' I'm going to my father's funeral – <u>come with me</u>.

Anna   Your father died?

Dan   It's fine, I hated him – no, I didn't – I don't <u>care</u>, I *care* about <u>THIS</u>.
Come with me, spend a weekend with me, then decide.

Anna   I don't want to go to your father's funeral.
There's nothing to . . . *<u>decide</u>*.
What about Alice?

Dan   She'll <u>survive</u>.

I can't be her father any more.

Anna, you want to believe he's . . . 'the one' . . . it's not *real*, you're scared of *<u>this</u>*.

Anna   There is no '<u>this</u>'. I <u>love</u> him.

Dan   *Why?*

Anna   Any number of reasons!

Dan   Name *one*.

Anna   He's kind.

Dan (*ferocious*)   Don't give me 'kind'. 'Kind' is *dull*, 'kind' will kill you. Alice is '*kind*', even *I'm* '<u>kind</u>,' anyone can be fucking KIND.

(*Gently.*) I cannot live without you.

Anna   You can . . . you *do*.

Beat.

Dan   This is not me, I don't do this.

All the language is old, there are no new words . . . *I love you.*

Beat.

Anna   No, you don't.

Dan   Yes . . . I do. I *need* you.
I can't think, I can't work, I can't *breathe*.
We are going to *<u>die</u>*.
Please . . . *save* me.

Look at me.

Anna *looks at* **Dan**.

Dan   Tell me you're not in love with me.

Beat.

Anna   I'm not in love with you.

Pause.

Dan   You just lied.
See me next week. *Please*, Anna . . . I'm begging you . . . *I'm*
your stranger . . . *jump*.

Silence. They are very close. **Larry** *has entered, he is looking at them.*
Dan *sees him and goes to exit.*

Anna   Your case.

Dan *returns, picks up his suitcase and exits.*

Pause.

Larry   Hallo . . . *Stranger*.

Anna   Hallo.

Larry   Intense conversation?

Beat.

Anna   His father's died. Were you *spying*?

Larry   Lovingly *observing* – (with a telescope).

He kisses **Anna**.

He's taller than his photo.

Anna   The photo's a head shot.

Larry   Yeah, I know, but his head *implied* a short body . . .
but in fact, his head is . . . deceptive.

Anna   Deceptive?

Larry Yes, because he's actually got a *long* body. He's a stringy fucker.

Anna *laughs*.

Larry I could 'ave 'im.

Anna *What?*

Larry If it came to it, in a scrap, I could 'ave 'im.

Anna *smiles*.

Larry Did you tell him we call him 'Cupid'?

Anna No, that's *our* joke.

Anna *tugs his sweater, pulling him towards her.*

Larry I've never worn cashmere before. Thank you. I'm Cinderella at the ball.

Anna (*charmed*) You're such a peasant.

Larry You love it.

He holds her.

I had a chat with young Alice.

Anna Fancy her?

Larry Course. Not as much as *you*.

Anna Why?

Larry You're a woman . . . she's a girl.
She has the moronic beauty of youth but she's got . . . *side*.

Anna She seems very open to me.

Larry That's how she *wants* to seem.
You forget you're dealing with a clinical observer of the human carnival.

Anna Am I now?

Larry Oh yes.

Anna   You seem more like 'the cat who got the cream'.
You can stop licking yourself, you know.

Pause. **Anna** *turns to* **Larry**, *slowly.*

Larry (*coolly*)   That's the nastiest thing you've ever said to
me.

Anna   God, I'm sorry. It was a <u>horrible</u> thing to say. It's
just . . . my family's here and friends . . .
I have no excuse. I'm sorry.

Pause.

Larry   Forget it. I know what you mean. I'll stop pawing
you.

Anna *kisses him.*

Larry   I met your *Dad* . . .

Anna   I know. He actually said, 'I like him.' He's never
said that before . . . about *anyone*. They all adored you; my
stepmother thinks you're gorgeous, 'Lovely hands,' she said,
'you can imagine him doing his stitching, very sensitively.'

Larry   So they didn't think I was 'beneath you'?

Anna   *No*. You're not . . . you're *you* and you're wonderful.

Larry *holds her.*

Larry   Did you like my folks? They loved *you*.

Anna   Your mother's got such a . . . kind face.

They look at each other.

Blackout.

Scene Six

Domestic interiors.

Midnight. June (a year later).

Anna *sitting on a chaise longue.*

Alice *asleep, curled up on a small sofa. She is wearing striped pyjamas. A half-eaten red apple beside her.*

They are in separate rooms.

Dan *enters. He carries the brown briefcase seen in Scene One.*
He looks at **Alice***.*
After a while she wakes.

Alice   Where've you been?

What?

Dan   Work. I had a drink with Harry. You never have *one* drink with Harry.

Alice   Did you eat? I made sandwiches – no crusts.

Dan   I'm not hungry.

Pause.

Alice   *What?*

Beat.

Dan   This will hurt.

I've been with Anna.

I'm in love with her. We've been seeing each other for a year.

Silence.

Alice *gets up and slowly exits.*

On the other side of the stage **Larry** *enters.*
He has a suitcase, bags, duty-free carrier.

Larry (*to* **Anna**)   Don't move!
I want to remember this moment for ever: the first time I walked through the door, returning from a business trip, to be greeted by my *wife*.
I have, in this moment, become an adult.

He kisses **Anna**.

Thanks for waiting up, you darling. You goddess.
I missed you.
Jesus, I'm knackered.

Anna   Didn't you sleep on the plane?

Larry   No, because the permed German sleeping next to
me was snoring like a *Messerschmitt*.

He removes his jacket, **Anna** *takes it.*

What's the time?

Anna   Midnight.

Larry   Seven.
Time: what a tricky little fucker.
My head's in two places, my brain actually *hurts*.

Anna   Do you want some food?

Larry   Nahh, I ate my 'Scooby Snacks' on the plane. I
need a bath.

Anna   Shall I run you one?

Larry   No, I'll just have a shower.

He untucks his shirt and kicks off his shoes.

You OK?

Anna   Mmhmm.

Beat. They look at each other.

How was the . . . *thing*?

Larry   As dermatological conferences go, it was a riot.

Larry *takes a bottle of Scotch from his bag of duty-free and swigs it.*

Anna   How was the hotel?

Larry   Someone told me that the beautiful people of '*The Paramount Hotel*', the concierge and the bell boys and girls – did you know this? They're all *whores*.

Anna   Everyone knows that.

Larry   *I* didn't. Want some?

He offers the bottle, **Anna** *takes a swig.*

I *love* New York. What a town: it's a twenty-four-hour pageant called, 'Whatever You Want.'
Then, you arrive back at Heathrow and the first thing you see is this . . . *carpet*.
This Unbelievable <u>Carpet</u>.
What the fuck colour is the carpet at Heathrow Airport? They must've laid it to reassure foreigners we're not a serious country.

God, I stink.

Anna   Are you all right?

Larry   Yeah. I don't suppose you fancy a friendly poke?

Beat.

Anna   I've just had a bath.

Larry   I'll see to myself then, in the *Elle Decoration* bathroom.

Anna   You chose that bathroom.

Larry   Yeah and every time I wash in it I feel *dirty*. It's *cleaner* than I am. It's got <u>attitude</u>. The mirror says, 'Who the fuck are you?'

Anna   You chose it.

Larry   Doesn't mean I like it. We shouldn't have . . . *this*.

Larry *gestures vaguely about the room.*

Anna   Are you experiencing bourgeois guilt?

Beat.

Larry (*sharp*)   Working-class guilt.

He looks at **Anna**.

Why are you dressed? If you've just had a bath.

Beat.

Anna   We needed some milk.

Larry   Right.

He goes to exit, stops.

You OK?

Anna   Uhhuh. You?

Larry   Yeah . . .

Larry *exits.*
Alice *enters. She is wearing the black coat from Scene One, also her rucksack from the same scene.*

Alice   I'm going.

Dan   I'm sorry.

Alice   <u>Irrelevant</u>. What are you sorry for?

Beat.

Dan   Everything.

Alice   Why didn't you tell me before?

Beat.

Dan   Cowardice.

Alice   Is it because she's clever?

Dan   No, it's because . . . she doesn't need me.

Pause.

Alice   Do you bring her here?

Dan   Yes.

Alice   She sits here?

Dan   Yes.

Beat.

Alice   Didn't she get *married*?

Dan   She stopped seeing me.

Beat.

Alice   Is that when we went to the country? To celebrate our third anniversary?

Dan   Yes.

Alice   <u>At least have the guts to look at me</u>.

Dan *looks at her.*

Alice   Did you phone her? To beg her to come back? When you went for your 'long, *lonely* walks'?

Dan   Yes.

Alice   You're a piece of shit.

Dan   Deception is brutal, I'm not pretending otherwise.

Alice   How . . . ? How does it *work*? How can you do this to someone?

Silence.

Dan   I don't know.

Alice   Not good enough, I'm going.

Dan *prevents her from leaving.*

Dan   It's late, it's not *safe* out there.

Alice   And it's *safe* in here?

Dan   What about your things?

Alice   I don't need 'things'.

Dan   Where will you go?

Alice   I'll disappear.

Larry *enters having had his shower. He is wearing a dressing-gown. He hands* **Anna** *a shoebox.*

Larry   'The Sultan' has returned bearing gifts.

Anna *opens the box and takes out the shoes.*

Dan *moves towards* **Alice**.

Alice   DON'T COME NEAR ME.

Anna (*to* **Larry**)   They're beautiful. Thank you.

Larry *kisses* **Anna**.

Larry   Hey, guess what, *Alice* was at the Paramount Hotel.

Anna   What?

Larry   They sell arty postcards in the lobby, I bought one to boost your sales.

Larry *takes a postcard from his dressing-gown pocket and reads the back.*

'Young Woman, London'.

He hands the postcard to **Anna**.

And . . . I checked for your book in 'The Museum of Modern Art'. It's *there*. Someone bloody bought one! This *student* with a ridiculous little beard, he was drooling over your photo on the inside cover – fancied you, the *Geek*. I was so proud of you – 'You've Broken New York.'

Anna   You're wonderful.

Larry   Don't ever forget it.

Larry *exits*.

Alice   Change your mind.

Please, change your mind.

Can I still see you?

Dan . . . can I still see you?

Answer me.

Dan   I can't see you. If I see you I'll never leave you.

Beat.

Alice   What will you do if *I* find someone else?

Dan   Be jealous.

Beat.

Alice   Do you still fancy me?

Dan   Of course.

Alice *shakes her head.*

Alice   You're lying. I've been '*you*'.

She starts to cry.

Hold me?

Dan *holds her.*

Alice   I amuse you but I bore you.

Dan   No. *No.*

Alice   You did love me?

Dan   I'll *always* love you. You changed my life. I hate hurting you.

Alice   So why are you?

Dan   Because . . . I'm selfish and I think I'll be happier with her.

Alice   You won't, you'll miss me. No one will ever love you as much as I do.

Dan   I know.

Pause.

Alice   Why isn't love enough?

I'm the one who leaves.

I'm supposed to leave *you*.

I'm the one who leaves.

She kisses **Dan**. *He responds. She breaks.*

Make some tea . . . *Buster.*

Dan *exits.*
Alice *and* **Anna** *are alone.*
Larry *enters. He is wearing trousers and the black cashmere seen in Scene Five.*

Anna   Why are you dressed?

Larry   Because I think you might be about to leave me and I didn't want to be wearing a dressing-gown.

I slept with someone in New York.
A whore.
I'm sorry.

Please don't leave me.

Beat.

Anna   Why?

Larry   For sex. I wanted *sex*. (I wore a condom.)

Beat.

Anna   Was it . . . good?

Larry *huffs and puffs.*

Larry   . . . Yes . . .

Anna   '*Paramount*' whore?

Larry   No . . . Forty . . . something Street.

Anna   Where did you go?

Larry   Her place.

Anna   Nice?

Larry   Not as nice as ours. I'm really sorry.

Pause.

Anna   Why did you tell me?

Larry   I couldn't lie to you.

Anna   Why not?

Larry   Because I love you.

Pause.

Anna   It's fine.

Larry   Really? *Why?*

Anna *looks at her shoes.*

Anna   Guilt present?

Larry   Love present. Something's wrong . . .

Anna . . .

Anna *turns to him.*

Larry   Are you leaving me?

Anna *nods.*

Larry   Why?

Anna   Dan.

Beat.

Larry   'Cupid'? He's our *joke.*

Anna   I love him.

Pause.

Larry   You're seeing him now . . .

Anna   Yes.

Larry   Since when?

Anna   Since my opening, last year. I'm disgusting.

Beat.

Larry   You're *phenomenal* . . . you're so . . . <u>clever</u>.
Why did you marry me?

Anna   I stopped seeing him, I wanted us to work.

Larry   Why did you tell me you wanted children?

Anna   Because I did.

Larry   And now you want children with him?

Anna   Yes – I don't know – I'm so sorry.

Pause.

Larry   <u>*Why?*</u>

Beat.

Anna   I need him.

Silence.

Larry   But . . . we're happy . . . aren't we?

Anna   Yes.

Beat.

Larry   Are you going to live with him?

Anna   Yes. You stay here, if you want to.

Larry   I don't give a FUCK about '<u>the spoils</u>'.

Alice *exits with her rucksack.*

Larry   You did this the day we <u>met</u>; let me *hang* myself for
your amusement. Why didn't you tell me the second I
walked in the door.

Anna   I was scared.

Larry   Because you're a <u>coward</u>. You spoilt <u>*bitch*</u>.

Dan *enters with two cups of tea, he sees* **Alice** *has gone. He exits
after her.*

Larry   Are you dressed because you thought I might hit you?

He moves towards **Anna**, *slowly*.

(*Close.*) What do you think I *am*?

Anna   I've been hit before.

Larry   Not by me.

He stands over **Anna**.

Is he a good fuck?

Anna   Don't do this.

Larry   Just answer the question. Is he *good*?

Beat.

Anna   Yes.

Larry   Better than me?

Anna   Different.

Larry   Better?

Anna   Gentler.

Larry   What does that mean?

Anna   You know what it means.

Larry   *Tell me.*

Anna   No.

Larry   I treat you like a whore?

Anna   Sometimes.

Larry   Why would that be?

Silence.

Anna   I'm sorry, you're –

Larry <u>Don't say it</u>, don't fucking say, 'You're too good for me.' I *am* – <u>but don't say it</u>.

He kneels to her.

(*Gently.*) Anna, you're making the mistake of your life. You're leaving me because you think you don't deserve happiness, but you do, Anna, you do . . .

He looks at her.

Did you have a bath because you had sex with him?

Anna *looks at him. He moves away from her.*

Larry So you didn't smell of him? So you'd feel less *guilty*?

And how do you *feel*?

Anna Guilty.

Beat.

Larry Did you ever love me?

Anna <u>*Yes*</u>.

Larry Big fucking deal.

Silence. **Larry** *breaks down.*

Anna . . . please, don't leave me . . . *please.*

Anna *holds* **Larry**.

On the other side of the stage **Dan** *re-enters and sits on the sofa.*

Larry Did you do it here?

Anna No.

Larry Why not?

He breaks from her.

(*Hard.*) Just tell me the truth.

Beat.

Anna Yes, we did it here.

Larry Where?

Beat.

Anna Here.

Larry On this?

He gestures to the chaise longue.

We had our first fuck on this.

Think of *me*?

When?

<u>When did you do it here</u>?

ANSWER THE QUESTION.

Beat.

Anna (*scared*) This evening.

Pause.

Larry Did you come?

Anna Why are you doing this?

Larry Because I want to know.

Beat.

Anna (*softly*) Yes . . . I came.

Larry How many times?

Anna Twice.

Larry How?

Anna First he went down on me and then we fucked.

Beat.

Larry Who was where?

Anna (*tough*) I was on top and then he <u>fucked me from
behind</u>.

Larry   And that's when you came the second time?

Anna   _Why is the sex so important_?

Larry   BECAUSE I'M A FUCKING CAVEMAN.

Did you touch yourself while he fucked you?

Anna   Yes.

Larry   You wank for him?

Anna   Sometimes.

Larry   And he does?

Anna   We do everything that people who have sex do.

Larry   You enjoy sucking him off?

Anna   _Yes_.

Larry   You like his cock?

Anna   I love it.

Larry   You like him coming in your face?

Anna   _Yes_.

Larry   What does it taste like?

Anna   It tastes like you but _sweeter_.

Larry   THAT's the _spirit_. Thank you. Thank you for your _honesty_.
Now fuck off and die. You fucked-up slag.

Blackout.

Act Two

Scene Seven

Lapdance club.

Late night. September (three months later).

Larry *is sitting. He is wearing a smart suit.*

Alice *is standing. She is wearing a short dress, wig and high heels. She has a garter round her thigh, there is cash in the garter.*

They are in a private room. Music in the distance.

Larry *gazes at her. She smiles. She is nice to him.*

Silence.

Larry   I love you.

Pause.

Alice   Thank you.

Beat.

Larry   What's this room called?

Alice   'The Paradise Suite'.

Larry   How many Paradise Suites are there?

Alice   Six.

Beat.

Larry   Do I have to pay you to talk to me?

Alice   No, but if you want to tip me it's your choice.

He takes out a twenty. She presents her leg. He puts the money in her garter.

Thank you.

Larry   I went to a place like this in New York.

This is *swish*.
Pornography has gone upmarket – BULLY FOR
ENGLAND.
This is honest *progress*, don't you think?

Alice   England always imports the best of America.

Larry   I used to come here twenty years ago . . . it was a
punk club . . . the stage was . . .

He can't remember, he gives up.

Everything is a Version of Something Else.

He takes a slug of his drink.

Twenty years ago, how old were *you*?

Alice   Four.

Larry   Christ, when I was in flares you were in nappies.

Alice   My nappies were flared.

Larry *laughs.*

Larry   You have the face of an angel.

Alice   Thank you.

Larry   What does your cunt taste like?

Alice   Heaven.

Beat.

Larry   How long you been doing this?

Alice   Three months.

Larry   Straight after he left you?

Alice   No one left me.

Beat. **Larry** *glances round the room.*

Larry   Been here already tonight?

Alice   Yes.

Larry   With who?

Alice   A couple. A man and a woman.

Larry   What did you do?

Alice   I stripped, I danced, I bent over.

Larry   You gave this *couple* a thrill?

Alice   I think so.

Larry   What d'you talk about?

Alice   This and that.

Larry   D'you tell the truth?

Alice   Yes and no.

Larry   Are you telling *me* the truth?

Alice   Yes.

Larry   And no?

Alice   I'm telling you the truth.

Larry   Why?

Alice   Because it's what you want.

Larry   <u>Yes</u>. *It's what I <u>want</u>*.

He stares at her.

Nice *wig*.

Alice   Thank you.

Larry   Does it turn you on?

Alice   Sometimes.

Larry   *Liar.* You're telling me it turns you on because you think that's what I want to <u>hear</u>. You think *I'm* turned on by it turning *you* on.

Alice   The thought of me *creaming* myself when I strip for strangers doesn't turn you on?

Larry   Put like that . . . yes.

She shows him her behind.

Are you flirting with me?

Alice   Maybe.

Larry   Are you *allowed* to flirt with me?

Alice   Sure.

Larry   Really?

Alice   No I'm not, I'm breaking all the rules.

Larry   You're mocking me.

She sits opposite him.

Alice   Yes, I'm allowed to flirt.

Larry   To prise my money from me.

Alice   To prise your money from you I can say or do as I please.

Larry   Except *touch*.

Alice   We are not allowed to touch.

Larry   Is that a good rule do you think?

Alice   Sometimes.

Beat.

Larry   Open your legs.

She does so.

Wider.

She does so. Pause. **Larry** *looks between her legs.*

What would happen if I touched you now?

Alice   I would call Security.

Larry   And what would they do?

Alice   They would ask you to leave and ask you not to come back.

Larry   And if I refused to leave?

Alice   They would remove you. This is a two-way mirror.

She nods in the direction of the audience.

There are cameras in the ceiling.

Beat. **Larry** *glances up and to the audience.*

Larry   I think it's best that I don't attempt to touch you.

He looks at her.

I'd like to touch you . . . *later.*

Alice   I'm not a whore.

Larry   I wouldn't pay.

He gazes at her.

Why the fuck did he leave you?

Beat.

Alice   What's your job?

Larry   A question, you've asked me a question.

Alice   So?

Larry   It's a chink in your armour.

Alice   I'm not wearing armour.

Larry   *Yes you are.*
I'm in the skin trade.

Alice   You own strip clubs?

Larry (*smiles*)   Do I look like the sort of man who owns strip clubs?

Alice   Yes.

Larry *looks in the mirror / audience.*

Larry   Define that look.

Alice   *Rich.*

Larry   Close your legs. I don't own strip clubs.

Alice   Do you own golf clubs?

Larry   <u>You know what I do</u>.

He stands.

Why are you calling yourself <u>Jane</u>?

Alice   Because it's my name.

Larry   <u>But we both know it isn't.</u>
You're all protecting your identities. The girl in there who calls herself 'Venus'. What's her *real* name?

Alice   Pluto.

Larry   You're cheeky.

Alice   Would you like me to stop being cheeky?

Larry   No.

Beat.

Alice   What's *your* name?

Larry *considers.*

Larry   Daniel.

Beat.

Alice   Daniel the Dermatologist.

Larry   I never told you my job.

Alice   I guessed.

Larry *looks at her.*

Larry (*close*)   You're *strong*.

There's another one in there (judging by the scars, a recent patient of 'Doctor Tit'), she calls herself 'Cupid'. Who's going to tell her Cupid was a bloke?

Alice   He wasn't a bloke, he was a little boy.

Pause.

Larry   I'd like you to tell me your name. *Please.*

He gives her £20.

Alice   Thank you. My name is Jane.

Larry   Your *real* name.

He gives her £20.

Alice   Thank you. My real name is Jane.

Larry   <u>Careful</u>.

He gives her £20.

Alice   Thank you. It's still Jane.

Larry   I've got another five hundred quid here.

He takes out the money.

Why don't I give you – <u>All</u> – <u>This</u> – <u>Money</u> – and you tell me what your Real Name is,

He raises her face towards his with the wad of notes.

<u>Alice</u>.

She tries to take the money. **Larry** *withdraws it.*

Alice   I promise.

Larry *gives her the money.*

Alice   Thank you. My real name is Plain – Jane – Jones.

Larry   I may be rich but I'm not stupid.

Alice   What a shame, 'Doc', I love 'em rich and stupid.

Larry   DON'T FUCK AROUND WITH ME.

Alice   I apologise.

Larry   *Accepted.* All the girls in this hellhole; the pneumatic robots, the coked-up baby dolls – and you're no different – you all use 'stage names' to con yourselves you're someone else so you don't feel <u>ashamed</u> when you show your <u>cunts</u> and <u>arseholes</u> to Complete Fucking Strangers.

I'm trying to have a conversation here.

Alice   You're out of cash, Buster.

Larry   I've paid for the room.

Alice   This is extra.

Pause.

Larry   We met last year.

Alice   Wrong girl.

Larry   I touched your face at Anna's . . . opening.

I know you're in grief. I know you're . . . '*destroyed*'.

TALK TO ME.

Alice   I am.

Larry   Talk to me in <u>real life</u>.

I didn't know you'd be here.

I know who you are.

I love your scar, I love everything about you that hurts.

Silence. **Larry** *slowly breaks down.*

She won't even see me . . .

You feel the same, I *know* you feel the same.

Alice   You can't cry here.

Larry   Hold me, let me hold you.

Larry *approaches her.*

Alice   We're not allowed to touch.

Pause.

Larry   Come home with me, Alice. It's *safe*. Let me look after you.

Alice   I don't need looking after.

Larry   *Everyone* needs looking after.

Alice   I'm not your revenge fuck.

Pause.

Larry   I'll pay you.

Alice   I don't need your money.

Larry   You *have* my money.

Alice   Thank you.

Larry   THANK YOU, THANK YOU. Is that some kind of <u>rule</u>?

Alice   I'm just being polite.

Pause. **Larry** *sits down.*

Larry   Get a lot of men in here, crying their guts out?

Alice   Occupational hazard.

Beat.

Larry   Have you ever desired a customer?

Alice   Yes.

Larry   Put me out of my misery, do you . . . desire *me*? Because I'm being pretty fucking honest about my feelings for *you*.

Alice   Your '*feelings*'?

Larry   Whatever.

Beat.

Alice   No. I don't desire you.

Pause.

Larry   Thank you. Thank you sincerely for your honesty. Next question: do you think it's possible you could perceive me as something other than a sad slot machine spewing out money?

Alice   That's the transaction; you're the customer, I'm the service.

Larry   Hey, we're in a <u>strip club</u>, let's not debate sexual politics.

Alice   *Debate?*

Larry   You're asking for a smack, gorgeous.

Alice   No I'm not.

Beat.

Larry   But you *are* gorgeous.

Alice   'Thank you.'

Pause. **Larry** *stands, straightens his tie, lights a cigarette.*

Larry   Will you lend me my cab fare?

Alice (*laughing*)   No.

Larry   I'll give it back to you tomorrow . . .

Alice   Company policy, you give *us* the money.

Larry   And what do we get in return?

Alice   We're nice to you.

Larry   'And We Get To See You Naked.'

Alice   It's beautiful.

Larry   <u>Except</u> . . . you think you haven't given us anything of yourselves.

You think because you don't love us or desire us or even <u>like</u> us you think you've <u>won</u>.

Alice   It's not a war.

Larry *laughs for some time.*

Larry   But you <u>do</u> give us something of yourselves: you give us . . . *imagery* . . . and we do with it what we will.

If you women could see one minute of our Home Movies – the shit that slops through our minds every day – you'd string us up by our balls, you really would.

You don't understand the territory.
Because you *are* the territory.

I could tell you to strip right now . . .

Alice   Yes. Do you want me to?

Larry   No.

Alice . . . tell me something *<u>true</u>*.

Alice   Lying is the most fun a girl can have without taking her clothes off. But it's better if you do.

Larry   You're cold. You're all cold at heart.

He stares into the two-way mirror.

WHAT D'YOU HAVE TO DO TO GET A BIT OF INTIMACY AROUND HERE?

Alice   Well, maybe next time I'll have worked on my intimacy.

Larry   No. I'll tell you what's going to <u>work</u>. What's going to <u>*work*</u> is that you're going to take your clothes off right now and you're going to turn around *very slowly* and bend over and touch the fucking floor for my viewing pleasure.

Alice   That's what you want?

Beat.

Larry   What else could I want?

Blackout.

Scene Eight

Restaurant.

Evening / lunchtime. October (a month later).

Dan *is sitting at a table with a drink. He is smoking. He waits.*
Anna *joins him.*

Anna   Sorry, I'm really sorry.

Dan *kisses her.*

Dan   What happened?

Anna   Traffic.

Anna *sits.*

Dan   You're flushed, you didn't need to run.

Anna *smiles.*

Anna   Have you ordered?

Dan   I ordered a menu about ten years ago.

Pause. **Dan** *looks at her.*

So . . . how was it?

Anna   Oh . . . fine.

Beat.

Dan   You had lunch?

Anna   Mmhmm.

Beat.

Dan   Where?

Beat.

Anna   Here, actually.

Dan   *Here?*

Anna   He chose it.

Dan   Then what?

Anna   Then we left.

Pause.

Dan   *And?*

Anna   There is no 'and'.

Dan   You haven't seen him for four months, there must be an 'and'.

Anna *shrugs.*

Dan   How is he?

Anna   Terrible.

Dan   How's his *dermatology?*

Anna   He is now in private practice.

Dan   How does he square that with his politics?

Anna   He's not much concerned with politics at present.

Beat.

Dan   Was he weeping all over the place?

Anna   Some of the time.

Dan (*genuine*)   Poor bastard.

Was he . . . 'difficult' . . . ?

Anna   Are you angry I saw him?

Dan   No, no, it's just . . . I haven't seen *Alice.*

Anna   You <u>can't</u> see Alice, you don't know where she is.

Dan   I haven't tried to find her.

Anna   He's been begging me to see him for months, you *know* why I saw him, I saw him so he'd . . . <u>*sign*</u>.

Dan   So has he signed?

Anna   *Yes.*

Dan   Congratulations. You are now a divorcee – double divorcee. Sorry.

He takes her hand.

How do you feel?

Anna   Tired.

Dan *kisses her hand,* **Anna** *kisses his.*

Dan   I love you. *And* . . . I need a piss.

Dan *exits.*

Anna *reaches into her bag and pulls out the divorce papers.*

Larry *enters.*

Larry *(sitting)*   Afternoon.

Anna   Hi.

Larry *looks around.*

Larry   I hate this place.

Anna   At least it's central.

Larry   I hate central. The centre of London's a theme park. I hate 'retro' and I hate the future. Where does that leave me?

He looks at her.

Come back.

Anna   You promised you wouldn't.

Larry   *Come back.*

Beat.

Anna   How's work?

Larry   Oh, Jesus. Work's shit, OK.

He looks around for a waiter.

(*Loud.*) Do they <u>have</u> waiters here?

Anna   They're all busy.

Larry   I love you. Please come back.

Anna   I'm not coming back.

She spreads the divorce papers on the table. **Larry** *stares at them.*

Sign this, please.

Larry   No pen.

Anna *hands him her pen.*

Anna   Pen.

Larry *takes her hand.*

Anna   Give me back my hand . . .

Larry *lets go.*

Anna   Sign.

Beat.

Larry   I'll sign it on one condition: we skip lunch, we go to my sleek, little surgery and we christen the patients' bed with our final fuck. I know you don't *want* to, I know you think I'm *sick* for asking – but that's what I'm asking – 'For Old Times' Sake', because I'm obsessed with you, because I can't get over you unless you . . . because I think on some small level you owe me *something*, for deceiving me so . . . *exquisitely*.

For all these reasons I'm *begging* you to give me your body. Be my whore and in return I will pay you with your liberty. If you do this I swear I will not contact you again – you know I'm a man of my word.

I will divorce you and, in time, consider the possibility of a friendship.

He stands.

I'm going to the bar. I assume you still drink vodka tonic?

Anna *nods.*

Larry *exits.*

Dan *returns and sits.*

Dan   Any sign of a waiter?

Anna   No.

Dan   Do you want some food?

Anna   I'm not hungry.

Dan *stares at her,* **Anna** *turns to him, slowly.*

Dan   You slept with him, didn't you?

Pause.

Anna   Yes. I'm . . . 'sorry' . . .

Dan *smiles.*

Dan   What do you expect me to do?

Anna   Understand . . . hopefully?

Beat.

Dan   Why didn't you lie to me?

Anna   We said we'd always tell each other the truth.

Dan   What's so great about the truth? Try lying for a change – it's the currency of the world.

Anna   Dan, I did what he wanted and now he will <u>leave us alone</u>.
I love *you*, I didn't give *him* anything.

Dan   Your body?

Dan *reaches for his cigarettes.*

Anna   If Alice came to you . . . *desperate* . . . with all that love still between you and she said she needed you to want her so that she could get over you, you would do it. I wouldn't like it either but I would forgive you because it's . . . a mercy fuck – a *sympathy* fuck. Moral rape, everyone does it. It's . . . *kindness.*

Dan   No, it's <u>cowardice</u>.
You don't have the guts to let him hate you.

Did you enjoy it?

Anna   *No.*

Dan   So you hated every second of it?

Anna *looks at* **Dan**.

Dan   Did you come?

Anna   No.

Dan   Did you fake it?

Anna   Yes.

Dan   Why?

Anna   To make him *think* I enjoyed it, why do you think?

Dan   If you were just his <u>*slag*</u> why did you give him the pleasure of thinking you'd enjoyed it?

Anna   Because that's what slags *do.*

Dan   You fake it with me?

Anna   Yes, yes I do. I fake one in three, all right?

Dan   Tell me the truth.

Pause.

Anna   *Occasionally* . . . I have faked it.
It's not important, you don't *make* me come. I <u>come</u> . . . you're . . . 'in the area' . . . providing valiant assistance.

Dan   You make *me* come.

Anna   You're a man, you'd come if the tooth fairy winked at you.

Beat.

Dan   You're late because you've come straight here from being with him.

Beat.

Anna   Yes.

Dan   Where was it?

Anna   His new surgery.

Beat.

Dan   Long session.

Anna *tries to touch him, he pulls away from her.*

Anna   Dan, please be bigger than . . . *jealous*. Please, be bigger.

Dan   What could be bigger than jealousy?

Long silence.

Anna   When we're making love, why don't you kiss me?
Why don't you like it when I say I love you?
I'm on your side. *Talk to me.*

Dan   It *hurts*. I'm ashamed. I know it's illogical and I do understand but *I hate you.*

I love you and I don't like other men <u>fucking</u> you, is that so weird?

Anna   No. YES. It was only <u>sex</u>.

Dan *(hard)*   If you can still fuck him you haven't left him.

(Softly.) It's gone . . . we're not innocent any more.

Anna   Don't stop loving me . . . I can see it draining out of you.
I'm sorry, it was a stupid thing to do. It meant *nothing*.
If you love me enough you'll forgive me.

Dan   Are you *testing* me?

Anna   *No*. Dan, I do understand.

Dan (*gently*)   No . . . *he* understands.

He looks at her.

All I can see is *him* all over you.

He's clever, your *ex*-husband . . . I almost admire him.

Silence.

Anna   Where are you?

Alice?

Dan (*smiles*)   I was reading the paper once. She wanted some attention. She crouched down on the carpet and pissed right in front of me.
Isn't that the most charming thing you've ever heard?

Anna (*tough*)   Why did you swear eternal love when all you wanted was a fuck?

Dan   I didn't just want a fuck, I wanted <u>you</u>.

Anna   You wanted excitement, love bores you.

Dan   No . . . it disappoints me.

I think you enjoyed it; he wheedles you into bed, the old jokes, the strange familiarity,
I think you had 'a whale of a time' and the truth is, I'll never know unless I ask <u>*him*</u>.

Anna   Well, why don't you?

Larry *returns to the table with two drinks. Vodka tonic for* **Anna**, *Scotch and dry for himself.*

Larry   Vodka tonic for the lady.

Anna (*to* **Larry**)   Drink your drink and then we'll go.

Larry *looks at her.*

Anna (*to* **Larry**)   I'm doing this because I feel guilty and because I pity you. You know that, don't you?

Larry   Yes.

Anna (*to* **Larry**)   Feel good about yourself?

Larry   No.

Larry *drinks.*

Dan (*to* **Anna**)   I'm sorry . . .

Anna (*to* **Dan**)   I didn't do it to hurt you. It's not all about *you.*

Dan (*to* **Anna**)   I know.
Let's go home . . .

Dan *and* **Anna** *kiss.*

I'll get us a cab.

Dan *exits.* **Larry** *sits.*

Larry   Will you tell him?

Anna   I don't know.

Larry (*helpful*)   Better to be truthful about this sort of thing . . .

Anna   Sign.

Beat.

Larry   I forgive you.

Anna   Sign.

Larry *signs.*

Blackout.

Scene Nine

Museum.

Afternoon. November (a month later).

A glass cabinet containing a life-size model of a Victorian child. A girl, dressed in rags. Behind her a model of a London street circa 1880s.

Alice *is alone. She is wearing a cashmere sweater. She is looking at the exhibit.*

She is holding a small package.

Larry *enters. He watches her.*

Larry 'Young Woman, London'.

Alice *turns.*

Larry Hallo, gorgeous.

Alice You're late, you old fart.

Larry Sorry.

They kiss, warmly.

You minx.

He tugs the sweater.

Alice 'The sacred sweater', I'll give it back.

Larry It suits you. Keep it.

Alice Thank you.

She hands him the package.

Happy birthday.

Larry Thank you.
I'm late because I walked through Postman's Park to get here . . . and I had a little look . . . at the memorial.

Alice Oh.

Larry Yeah . . . *oh.*

Larry *looks at the exhibit, smiles.*

Alice   Do you hate me?

Larry   No, I adore you.

Alice   Do we have to talk about it?

Larry   Not if you don't want to.

She kisses him.

Alice   Thank you. I've got a surprise for you.

Larry   You're full of them.

Alice *looks at* **Larry**'s *watch.*

Alice   Wait here.

Alice *exits.*
Larry *opens the package, looks inside, smiles.*

Anna *enters looking at her watch. She has a guide book, camera and a large brown envelope. She is wearing the shoes* **Larry** *gave her in Scene Six.*
She sees **Larry**. *Stops.* **Larry** *looks up, sees her.*

Anna   What are *you* doing here?

Larry   I'm . . . lazing on a Sunday afternoon. You?

Anna   I'm meeting Alice.

Beat.

Larry   Who?

Anna   Dan's Alice – Dan's ex-Alice. She phoned me at the studio this morning . . . she wants her negatives . . .

Larry   . . . Right . . .

Beat.

Anna   You don't go to museums.

Larry   The evidence would suggest otherwise.

Beat.

Anna (*suspicious*)   Are you OK?

Larry   Yeah, you?

Anna   Fine. It's your birthday today.

Larry   I know.

Beat.

Anna   I thought of you this morning.

Larry   Lucky me.

Beat.

Anna   Happy birthday.

Larry   Thank you.

Anna *nods to the package.*

Anna   Present?

Larry (*evasive*)   . . . *Yeah* . . .

Anna   What is it?

Larry   A Newton's Cradle.

Anna   Who from?

Beat.

Larry   My dad.

Anna   From *Joe*?

Pause.

Larry   It's from *Alice*.

I'm fucking her.

I – Am – Fucking – Alice.

She's set us up, I had no idea you were meeting her.

Pause.

Anna   You're old enough to be her ancestor.

Larry   Disgusting, isn't it.

Anna   You should be ashamed.

Larry (*smiles*)   Oh, I am.

Beat.

Anna   . . . *How?*

Larry (*vague*)   I went to a club, she happened to be there.

Anna   A *club?*

Larry   Yeah, a club.

Anna   You don't go to clubs.

Larry   I'm reliving my youth.

Anna   Was it a strip club?

Larry   You know, I can't remember.

He looks at **Anna**.

Jealous?

Anna *shrugs*.

Larry   Ah, well.

Anna   When did it start?

Larry   About a month ago.

Anna   <u>Before</u> or <u>after</u> I came to your surgery?

Larry   The night before. (*Dirty.*) She made me strip for her.

Anna   I don't want to know.

Larry   I know.

Did you tell your 'soulmate' about *that* afternoon?

Anna   Of course.

Larry   How did he take it?

Beat.

Anna   Like a _man_.

She looks at him.

Larry   I told you it was best to be truthful.

Anna   You're sly.

Larry   Am I?

(*Fondly.*) You love your guide books, you look like a tourist.

Anna   I feel like one. Please don't hate me.

Larry   It's easier than loving you.

He looks at **Anna**.

Me and Alice . . . it's *nothing*.

Anna   Nice nothing?

Larry   Very.

They look at each other, close.

Since we're talking, could you have a word with your lawyer?
I'm still waiting for confirmation of our divorce.
If that's what you want.

Alice *enters.*

Alice   Hi, do you two know each other?

Larry   I think I'll leave you to it.

Alice   Good idea, we don't want *him* here while we're working, do we?

Larry (*to* **Alice**)   Later, Minx.
(*To* **Anna**.) Bye.

He makes to exit, turns.

(*To* **Anna**.) Nice shoes by the way.

Larry *exits.*

Anna   How did you get so brutal?

Alice   I lived a little.

Alice *strokes the sweater,* **Anna** *watches her.*

Anna   You're primitive.

Alice   Yeah, I am. How's Dan?

Anna   Fine.

Alice   Did you tell him you were seeing me?

Anna   No.

Alice   Do you cut off his crusts?

Anna   What?

Alice   Do you cut off his crusts?

Anna   What do you want?

Alice   I want my negatives.

Anna *hands the envelope to* **Alice**.

Alice   What's your latest project, Anna?

Anna   Derelict buildings.

Alice   How nice, the beauty of ugliness.

Anna   What are you doing with Larry?

Alice   *Everything.*

I like your bed.

You should come round one night, come and watch your
husband blubbering into his pillow – it might help you
develop a conscience.

Anna   I know what I've done.

Alice   His big thing at the moment is how upset his family are. Apparently, they all worship you, they can't understand why you had to ruin everything. He spends *hours* staring up my <u>arsehole</u> like there's going to be some answer there. Any ideas, Anna?

Why don't you go back to him?

Anna   And then Dan would go back to you?

Alice   Maybe.

Anna   *Ask* him.

Alice   I'm not a beggar.

Anna   Dan left you, I didn't force him to go.

Alice   You made yourself available, don't weasel out of it.

Anna   Screwing Larry was a big mistake.

Alice   Yeah, well, *everyone* screws Larry round here.

Anna   You're Dan's little girl, he won't like it.

Alice   <u>So don't tell him</u>, I think you owe me that.

Anna *looks away.*

Alice   She even looks beautiful when she's angry. The Perfect Woman.

Anna   JUST FUCKING STOP IT.

Alice   Now we're talking.

Anna   Why *now*, why come for me *now*?

Alice   Because I felt strong enough, it's taken me five months to convince myself you're not better than me.

Anna   It's not a competition.

Alice   <u>Yes it is</u>.

Anna   I don't want a fight.

Alice   SO GIVE IN.

Silence. They look at each other.

(*Gently.*) Why did you do this?

Anna (*tough*)   I fell in love with him, Alice.

Alice   That's the most stupid expression in the world.
'I fell in love' – as if you had no *choice*.
There's a moment, there's always a *moment*; I can do this, I
can give in to this or I can resist it. I don't know when your
moment was but I bet there was one.

Anna   Yes, there was.

Alice   You didn't fall in love, you gave in to temptation.

Anna   Well, *you* fell in love with him.

Alice   No, I *chose* him. I looked in his briefcase and I found
this . . . *sandwich* . . . and I thought, 'I will give all my love to
this charming man who cuts off his crusts.' I didn't *fall* in
love, I chose to.

Anna   You still want him, after everything he's done to
you?

Alice   You wouldn't understand, he . . . *buries* me.
He makes me invisible.

Anna (*curious*)   What are you *hiding* from?

Alice (*softly*)   Everything. Everything's a lie, nothing
matters.

Anna   Too easy, Alice. It's the cop-out of the age.

Alice   Yeah, well, you're *old*.

Anna *smiles to herself, looks at* **Alice**.

Anna   I am sorry. I had a choice and I chose to be selfish.
I'm sorry.

Alice (*shrugs*)   Everyone's selfish, I stole Dan from someone
else.

Anna   *Ruth?*

Alice   Ruth. She went to pieces when he left her.

Anna   Did *she* ever come and see *you*?

Alice   No.

She turns to **Anna**.

So . . . what are you going to do?

Anna   *Think*.

She touches **Alice**'s *sweater*.

Is Larry nice to you, in bed?

Alice   OK, Dan's better.

Anna   Rubbish, at least Larry's *there*.

Alice   Dan's there, in his own quiet way.

Anna   They spend a lifetime fucking and never know how to make love.

Pause.

Alice   I've got a scar on my leg, Larry's mad about it, he licks it like a dog. Any ideas?

Anna (*shrugs*)   *Dermatology*? God knows. This is what we're dealing with.

We arrive with our . . . 'baggage' and for a while they're brilliant, they're 'Baggage Handlers'.
We say, 'Where's *your* baggage?' They deny all knowledge of it . . . '*They're in love*' . . . they have none.
Then . . . just as you're relaxing . . . a Great Big Juggernaut arrives . . . with <u>their</u> baggage.
It Got Held Up.

They love the way we make them *feel* but not 'us'.
They love dreams.

Alice   So do we. You should lower your expectations.

Anna   It's easy to say that. I'm not being patronising but you're a child.

Alice   You are being patronising.

Anna   And you *are* a child.

They look at each other.

Who's '*Buster*'?

Alice   'Buster'? No idea.

Anna   He says it in his sleep.

Alice (*smiles*)   I've got to go.

Alice *makes to exit.*

Anna   Don't forget your negatives.

Alice *picks up the envelope.*

Alice   Oh, yeah. Thanks.

She hands the envelope to **Anna**.

Do the right thing, Anna.

Alice *exits.* **Anna** *looks at the envelope.*

Blackout.

Scene Ten

Larry's *surgery.*

Late afternoon. December (a month later).

On **Larry**'s *desk: computer, phone, a Newton's Cradle. Also in the room, a surgery bed.* **Larry** *is seated at his desk.*
Dan *is standing, distraught. He holds his brown briefcase.*

Silence.

Larry   So?

Dan   I want Anna back.

Larry   She's made her choice.
You look like *shit*.

Beat. **Dan** *puts his briefcase down.*

Dan   I owe you an apology. I fell in love with her.
My intention was not to make you suffer.

Larry   Where's the apology? You <u>cunt</u>.

Dan   I apologise.

If you love her, you'll let her go so she can be . . . happy.

Larry   She doesn't want to be 'happy'.

Dan   Everyone wants to be happy.

Larry   Depressives don't. They want to be *unhappy* to
confirm they're depressed. If they were <u>happy</u> they couldn't
be depressed any more, they'd have to go out into the world
and *<u>live</u>*, which can be . . . *depressing*.

Dan   Anna's not a depressive.

Larry   Isn't she?

Dan   I love her.

Larry   Boo hoo, so do I. You don't love Anna, you love
yourself.

Dan   You're *wrong*, <u>I don't love myself</u>.

Larry   Yes you do, and you know something; you're
winning – you selfish people – it's *your* world. *<u>Nice</u>*, isn't it?

Dan *glances round the sleek surgery.*

Dan   *Nice* office.
It's *you* who's selfish. You don't even want *Anna*, you want
<u>revenge</u>.

She's gone back to you because she can't bear your *suffering*. You don't know who she is, you love her like a dog loves its owner.

Larry   And the owner loves the dog for so doing. Companionship will always triumph over '*passion*'.

Dan   You'll hurt her, you'll never forgive her.

Larry   Of course I'll forgive her – I *have* forgiven her. Without forgiveness we're savages. You're <u>*drowning*</u>.

Dan   You only *met* her because of me.

Larry   Yeah . . . *thanks*.

Dan   It's a joke, your marriage to her is a <u>joke</u>.

Larry   Here's a good one: she never sent the divorce papers to her lawyer.

To a 'Towering Romantic Hero' like you I don't doubt I'm somewhat common but I am, nevertheless, what she has chosen.

And we must respect What The Woman Wants.

If you go *near* her again, I promise –

The phone rings.

– I will kill you.

He picks it up.

(*In phone.*) Uh-huh. OK.

He puts the phone down.

I have patients to see.

He takes his jacket off to prepare for his patient.

Dan   When she came here you think she enjoyed it?

Larry   I didn't fuck her to give her a '*nice time*'. I fucked her to fuck you up. A good fight is never clean.

And yeah, she enjoyed it, as you know, she loves a guilty fuck.

Dan   You're an animal.

Larry   YES. What are _you_?

Dan   You think love is simple? You think the heart is like a diagram?

Larry   Ever _seen_ a human heart? It looks like a fist wrapped in blood.
GO FUCK YOURSELF . . . you . . . _WRITER_. You <u>LIAR</u>.
Go check a few facts while I get my hands dirty.

Dan   She hates your hands. She hates your simplicity.

Pause.

Larry   <u>Listen</u> . . . I've spent the whole week talking about _you_.

Anna tells me you fucked her with your eyes closed.
She tells me you wake in the night, crying for your dead mother.

You mummy's boy.

Shall we stop this?

It's _over_. Accept it.

You don't know the first thing about love because you don't understand _compromise_.

You don't even know . . . _Alice_.

Dan _looks at him._

Larry   Consider her scar, how did she get that?

Beat.

Dan   When did _you_ meet Alice?

Pause.

Larry   Anna's exhibition. _You_ remember.

A scar in the shape of a question mark, solve the mystery.

Dan   She got it when her parents' car crashed.

Pause.

Larry   There's a condition called '*dermatitis artefacta*'. It's a mental disorder manifested in the skin. The patient manufactures his or her very own skin disease. They pour bleach on themselves, gouge their skin, inject themselves with their own piss, sometimes their own shit. They create their own disease with the same diabolical attention to detail as the artist or the lover. It looks 'real' but its source is the deluded self.

He takes a roll of paper and makes a new sheet on the surgery bed.

I think Alice mutilated herself.
It's fairly common in children who lose their parents young.
They blame themselves, they're disturbed.

Dan   Alice is not 'disturbed'.

Larry   <u>But she *is*</u>.
You were so busy feeling your grand artistic '*feelings*' you couldn't see what was in front of you. The girl is fragile and tender. She didn't want to be put in a book, she wanted to be *loved*.

Dan   How do *you* know?

Beat.

Larry   Clinical observation.

*He hands **Dan** his briefcase indicating for him to leave.*
*He looks at **Dan**, close.*

Don't cry on me.

*Silence. **Dan** breaks down, uncontrollably. **Larry** observes him.*

Dan   I'm sorry.

He continues to cry.

I don't know what to do.

Larry *watches him sob. Eventually . . .*

Larry   Sit down.

Dan *sinks into a chair, head in hands.*

Larry   You want my advice? Go back to her.

Dan   She'd never have me. She's vanished.

Pause.

Larry   No, she hasn't.

Dan *looks up.*

Larry   I found her . . . by accident. She's working in . . . a
. . . 'club'.
Yes, I saw her naked.
No, I did not fuck her.

Dan   You spoke to her?

Larry   Yes.

Dan   What about?

Larry   *You.*

The phone rings. **Larry** *picks it up. He hands* **Dan** *a Kleenex.*

(*In phone.*) Yes. One minute.

Larry *puts the phone down. He writes on his prescription pad.*

Dan   How is she?

Larry (*writing*)   She loves you. Beyond Comprehension.
Here . . . your prescription.

He hands **Dan** *a piece of paper.*

It's where she works.

<u>Go to her</u>.

They look at each other.

Dan   Thank you.

Larry *starts to consult his files.*
Dan *moves to leave but then gestures to the Newton's Cradle.*

Dan   Where did you get that?

Larry   A present.

He begins to work on his computer.

Still pissing about on the Net?

Dan   Not recently.

Beat.

Larry   I wanted to *kill* you.

Dan   I thought you wanted to *fuck* me.

Larry (*smiles*)   Don't get lippy.
I liked your book by the way.

Dan   Thanks . . . You Stand Alone.

Larry   *With Anna.*

You should write another one.

Dan (*shrugs*)   Haven't got a subject.

Beat.

Larry   When I was nine, a policeman touched me up.
He was my uncle. Still *is*. Uncle Ted.
Nice bloke, married, bit of a demon darts player.

Don't tell me you haven't got a subject, every human life is
a million stories.

Thank God life *ends* – we'd never survive it.

From Big Bang to weary shag, the history of the world.

Our flesh is ferocious . . . our bodies will kill us . . . our
bones will outlive us.

Still writing obituaries?

Dan   Yes.

Larry   Busy?

Dan (*nods*)   I was made editor.

Larry   Yeah? How come?

Dan   The previous editor died.

They smile.

Alcohol poisoning. I sat with him for a week, in the hospital.

They look at each other.

Larry   I really do have patients to see.

Dan *gestures to the Newton's Cradle.*

Dan   Alice . . . gave me one of those.

Larry   Really?

Beat.

Dan   And yours?

Larry   My dad.

Dan (*suspicious*)   Your father?

Larry   Yeah, he loves old tat.

Dan   He's a cab driver, isn't he?

Larry   Yeah.

He points to **Dan** *indicating, 'and yours'.*

. . . Teacher?

Dan   History.

Pause. **Larry** *sets the cradle in motion. They watch it moving.*

Larry   You should never have messed with Anna.

Dan *gets up.*

Dan   I know, I'm sorry. Thank you.

Larry   For what?

Dan   Being kind.

Larry   I am kind. Your invoice is in the post.

Dan *goes to exit.*

Larry   Dan . . .

Dan *turns to* **Larry**.

Larry   I lied to you.

I did fuck Alice.

I'm sorry for telling you.

I'm just . . . not . . . *big enough* to forgive you.

Buster.

They look at each other.

Blackout.

Scene Eleven

Hotel room.

Late night. January (a month later).

Dan *is lying on the bed, smoking. He is reading a Gideon's Bible. He stubs his cigarette in the ashtray.*
Alice *is in the bathroom offstage.*

Alice (*off*)   SHOW ME THE SNEER.

Dan *sneers in the direction of the bathroom.*

Alice (*off*)   BOLLOCKS.

Dan (*laughing*)   It's two in the morning, you'll wake the hotel.

Alice *enters in her pyjamas. She cartwheels on to the bed.*

Alice   Fuck me!

Dan   *Again*? We have to be up at six.

Alice   How can *one* man be so endlessly disappointing?

Dan   That's my *charm*.

Alice *lies in his arms.*

Dan   So . . . where are we going?

Alice   My treat – my holiday surprise – my rules.

Dan *tickles her.*

Dan   <u>Where</u> are we *going*?

Alice (*laughing*)   New York.

Dan   You angel.
How long's the flight?

Alice   Seven hours.

Dan   I can't fly for seven hours.

Alice   The *plane* will do the flying. I'll protect you.

She kisses him.

Don't be scared of flying.

Dan   I'm not, I'm scared of *crashing*. Did you remember to pack my passport?

Alice   Of course, it's with my passport.

Dan   And where's that?

Alice   In a place where *you* can't look. *No one* sees my passport photo.

Dan *strokes her.*

Alice   Hey, when we get on the plane we'll have been together four years.
Happy anniversary . . . *Buster*.

Dan *stops, looks at her.*

Dan   I'm going to take my eyes out.

Alice   Brush your teeth as well.

Dan *gets off the bed.*

Dan   What was in my sandwiches?

Alice   Tuna.

Dan   What colour was my apple?

Alice   Green.

Dan   It was *red*.

Alice   It was *green* and it was horrible.

Dan   What were your first words to me?

Alice   'Hallo, Stranger.'

Dan   What a slut.

Beat.

Alice   Where had I been?

Dan   'Clubbing', then the meat market and then . . . the buried river.

Beat.

Alice   The what?

Dan   You went to Blackfriars Bridge to see where the Fleet river comes out . . . *the swimming pig* . . . all that.

Alice   You've lost the plot, *Grandad*.

Dan *'remembers' and exits to the bathroom.*

Dan (*off*)   And you went to that park . . . with the memorial.

Alice   Who did *you* go there with?

Dan (*off*)   My old dead dad.

Alice   He ate an egg sandwich, he had butter on his chin.

Dan (*off*)   How do you *remember* these things?

Alice   Because *my* head's not full of specky, egghead <u>rubbish</u>.
What was your euphemism?

Dan (*off*)   Reserved. Yours?

Alice   Disarming. Were the chairs red or yellow?

Dan *enters. He is now wearing his spectacles.*

Dan   No idea.

Alice   Trick question, they were orange.

Dan   *You* are a trick question. *Damsel.*

Alice   *Knight.*

Alice *opens her legs.* **Dan** *looks at her, remembers something.*

Pause.

Dan   Do you remember a doctor?

Beat.

Alice   No . . . what doctor?

Pause.

Dan   There was a *doctor* . . . he gave you a cigarette.

Beat.

Alice   No. I haven't been on holiday for . . . *ever.*

Dan   We went to the country.

Alice   That doesn't count, you were making sneaky calls to that . . . *witch* we do not mention.

Dan *watches her.*

Dan   Do you think they're happy?

Alice   Who?

Dan   Anna and . . . *Larry.*

Alice   Couldn't give a toss. Come to bed.

Dan   I want a *fag.* How did *you* manage to give up?

Alice   Deep Inner Strength.

Dan *gets into bed. He holds* **Alice***, kisses her, strokes her leg.*

Dan   How *did* you get this?

Alice   You know how.

Dan   How?

Alice   I fell off my bike because I refused to use stabilisers.

Dan (*disbelieving*)   Really?

Alice   You know how I got it.

Beat.

Dan   Did you do it yourself?

Alice   No.

Beat.

Dan   Show me your passport.

Alice   No, I look ugly.

Beat.

Dan   When are you going to stop stripping?

Alice   Soon.

Dan   You're *addicted* to it.

Alice   No I'm not.

It paid for this.

Pause. **Dan** *struggles but can't stop himself.*

Dan   Tell me what happened.

Alice   Dan . . . *don't.* Nothing happened.

Dan   But he came to the club?

Alice   Loads of men came to the club. *You* came to the club. The look on your face.

Dan   The look on *your* face.
What a face. What a *wig*.

He gazes at her.

I *love* your face . . . I saw *this* face . . . this . . . *vision.*
And then you stepped into the road.
It was the moment of my life.

Alice   *This* is the moment of your life.

Dan   You were perfect.

Alice   I still am.

Dan   I know.

On the way to the hospital . . . when you were '*lolling*' . . . I kissed your forehead.

Alice   You brute!

Dan   The cabbie saw me kiss you . . . he said, 'Is she yours?' and I said, 'Yes . . . she's *mine.*'

He kisses her forehead, holds her close. Struggles with himself.

So he came to the club, watched you strip, had a little chat and that was it?

Alice   Yes.

Dan   You're not *trusting* me. I'm in love with you, you're *safe*. If you fucked him you fucked him, I just <u>want to know</u>.

Alice   Why?

Dan (*tenderly*)   Because I want to know *everything* because . . . I'm . . . *insane.*

He strokes her face. Pause.

<u>*Tell me*</u> . . .

Long silence.

Alice   Nothing happened. You were living with someone else.

Dan (*sharp*)   What are you justifying?

Alice   I'm not justifying anything . . . I'm just *saying*.

Dan   What are you <u>saying</u>?

Alice   I'm not saying anything.

Dan   <u>I</u> <u>just</u> <u>want</u> <u>the</u> <u>truth</u>.

Dan *gets out of bed and puts his trousers on.*

Alice   I'm telling you the truth.

Dan   You and the truth are known strangers.

Did you ever give him a present?

Beat.

Alice   No. Where are you going?

Dan   Cigarettes.

Alice   Everywhere's closed.

Dan   I'll go to the terminal, I'll be back soon.

He puts his coat on.

When I get back *please* tell me the truth.

Alice   Why?

Dan   Because I'm addicted to it. Because without it we're animals. Trust me, I love you.

He looks at her.

What?

Alice *slowly turns to him.*

Silence.

Alice   I don't love you any more.

Pause.

Dan   Look . . . I'm sorry . . .

Alice   No, I've changed the subject. I don't love you any more.

Dan   Since when?

Alice (*gently*)   Now . . . Just Now.

I don't want to lie and I can't tell the truth so it's over.

Dan   Alice . . . don't leave me.

Alice *gets out of bed and goes to her rucksack, she finds* **Dan***'s passport and hands it to him.*

Alice   I've left . . . I've *gone.*
'I don't love you any more. Goodbye.'

Beat.

Dan   Why don't you tell me the truth?

Alice (*softly*)   So you can hate me?
I fucked Larry. Many times. I enjoyed it. I came. I prefer *you.* Now go.

Pause.

Dan   I knew that, he told me.

Alice   You *knew?*

Dan   I needed *you* to tell me.

Alice   *Why?*

Dan   Because he might've been lying, I had to hear it from *you.*

Alice   I would never have told you because I know you'd never forgive me.

Dan   I would, I *have!*

Alice   Why did he tell you?

Dan   Because he's a <u>bastard</u>!

Alice (*distraught*)   How could he?

Dan   Because he wanted <u>this</u> to happen.

Alice   But why *test* me?

Dan   <u>Because I'm an idiot</u>.

Alice   *Yeah.*

I would've loved you for ever. Now, please go.

Dan   Don't do this, Alice, talk to me.

Alice   I'm talking – *fuck off.*

Dan   I'm sorry, you misunderstand, I didn't mean to –

Alice   Yes you did.

Dan   *I love you.*

Alice   <u>*Where*</u>*?*

Dan   What?

Alice   *Show me.* Where is this '<u>*love*</u>'?
I can't see it, I can't *touch* it, I can't *feel* it.
I can <u>hear</u> it, I can hear some <u>*words*</u> but I can't *do* anything
with your easy words.

Dan   Listen to me, please –

Alice   Whatever you say it's too late.

Dan (*desperately*)   *Please* don't do this.

Alice   <u>It's done</u>. Now <u>go</u> or I'll call . . . *security.*

Beat.

Dan   You're not in a strip club. There is no security.

They look at each other. Pause.

Alice *tries to grab the phone.* **Dan** *throws her on to the bed. They struggle.*

Dan   Why d'you fuck him?

Alice   I wanted to.

Dan   *Why?*

Alice   I *desired* him.

Dan   *Why?*

Alice   *You* weren't there.

Dan   Why <u>him</u>?

Alice   He asked me nicely.

Dan   <u>You're a liar</u>.

Alice   So?

Dan   WHO ARE YOU?

Alice   I'M NO ONE.

She spits in his face. He grabs her by the throat, one hand.

Alice   Go on, hit me. That's what you *want*. <u>Hit me, you fucker</u>.

Silence.

Dan *hits* **Alice**, *a slap across her face.*

Silence.

Alice   Do you have a single original thought in your head?

Blackout.

Scene Twelve

Postman's Park.

Afternoon. July (six months later).

A summer's day. **Anna** *is looking at the memorial. She has a guide book.*
Larry *stands, holding his white coat. He carries two styrofoam cups. He watches her. She turns.*

Anna *Spy.*

Larry *approaches.*

Anna You've got the coat.

Larry The white coat.

Anna Hallo, Doctor Larry.

Larry *hands a cup to* **Anna**.

Anna Thanks. Have you read these?

Anna *turns back to the memorial.*

Larry Yeah, I knew you'd like it.

Larry *sits on a park bench and lights a cigarette.*

Anna (*reading*) 'Elizabeth Boxall . . . aged seventeen . . . who died of injuries received in trying to save a child from a runaway horse. June 20th 1888.'

She turns to **Larry**.

How's Polly?

Beat.

Larry Polly's great.

Anna I always knew you'd end up with a pretty nurse.

Larry Yeah? How?

Anna I just thought you would.

Is she . . . 'the one'?

Larry I don't know.

He glances at **Anna**.

No.

Everyone learns, nobody changes.

Anna   *You* don't change.

Beat.

Larry   You . . . seeing anyone?

Anna   No.

I got a dog.

Larry   Yeah? What sort?

Anna   Mongrel, she's a stray. I found her in the street, no collar . . . nothing.

Pause.

Larry   You look fantastic.

Anna   Don't *start*.

Larry   I'd give you one . . .

Anna *looks at him.*

Larry   Serious.

Anna   Fuck off and die, you fucked-up slag.

Pause.

Larry   I never told you this: when I strode into the bathroom . . . *that night* . . . I banged my knee on our cast-iron tub. The bathroom *ambushed* me. While you were sobbing in the sitting room I was hopping around in agony. The mirror was having a field day.

Anna *smiles.*

Larry   How's work?

Anna   I'm having a break . . . I'm taking the dog to the country . . . we're going to go for long walks.

Beat.

Larry   Don't become . . . a sad person.

Anna   I won't. I'm *not*. <u>Fuck off</u>.

Larry *looks at her.*

Larry   Don't give your love to a dog.

Anna   Well, *you* didn't want it, in the end.

There's always someone younger.

They look out at the memorial.

Silence.

Larry   How did she die?

Anna   I don't know. When he phoned, he said it
happened last night in New York.
He's flying out today and he wanted to see us before he left.

Larry   So they weren't together?

Anna   They split up in January.

Beat.

Larry   Did he say why?

Anna   No.

Beat.

Larry   How did they contact him?

Anna   Maybe she wrote his name in her passport as 'next
of kin'.
You're still in mine – 'in the event of death'.
I must remove you.

Are you glad you're back at the hospital?

She sits with **Larry**.

Larry   Yeah. Well, Polly said she wouldn't have sex with
me until I gave up private medicine. What's a man to do?

Anna *looks at the memorial.*

Anna   Do you think the families arranged these?

Larry   I suppose. It's like putting flowers at the roadside. People need to remember.
It makes things seem less . . . random.

Actually, I hate this memorial.

Anna   Why?

Larry   It's the sentimental act of a Victorian philanthropist: remember the dead, forget the living.

Anna   You're a pompous bastard.

Larry   And *you* are an incurable romantic.

Have a look for Alice Ayres.

Anna   Larry, that's horrible.

Larry *points to one memorial in particular.*

Larry (*reading*)   'Alice Ayres, daughter of a bricklayer's labourer, who by intrepid conduct saved three children from a burning house in Union Street, Borough, at the cost of her own young life.

April 24th 1885.'

She made herself up.

They look at the memorial.
After a while, **Larry** *puts his cigarette out and picks up his white coat.*

I'm not being callous but I've got a lot of patients to see. Will you give my apologies to Dan? I'm not good at grief.

Anna   You're a coward.

Larry   I know.

Anna *continues to look at the memorial then turns to* **Larry**.

Anna   You do remember me?

They look at each other.

Dan *enters. He is wearing the suit and carrying the suitcase seen in Scene Five. He is holding a bunch of flowers. He is exhausted.*

Dan   I couldn't get away from work, sorry.

Larry   Dan . . . I'm sorry . . . I have to . . .

Dan   It's fine.

Larry *exits.*

Dan (*to* **Anna**)   You look well.

Anna   I am well.

Dan *looks out at the memorial.*

Anna   Dan . . .

Anna *gestures for him to sit, he remains standing.*

Dan   This is where we sat.

Anna   Who?

Dan   Me and my father, didn't I tell you?

Anna   No, wrong girl, you told Alice.

Beat.

Dan   *Jane.* Her name was Jane Jones.

The police phoned me . . . they said that someone I knew, called Jane, had died . . . (they found her address book).

I said there must be a mistake . . .

They had to *describe* her.

There's no one else to identify the body.

She was knocked down by a car . . . on Forty-third and Madison.

When I went to work today . . . Graham said, 'Who's on the slab?'

I went out to the fire escape and just . . . cried like a baby.

I covered my face – why do we do that?

A man from the Treasury had died.
I spent all morning . . . writing his obituary.

There's no space. There's not enough . . . *space*.

He sits on the bench with **Anna**.

The phone rang. It was the police . . . they said there's no
record of her parents' death . . . they said they were trying
to trace them.

She told me that she fell in love with me because . . . I cut
off my crusts . . . but it was just . . . it was only *that* day . . .
because the bread . . . *broke* in my hands.

He turns away from **Anna**, *looks at the flowers*.

Silence.

He turns back to **Anna**.

I bumped into *Ruth*.

She's married. One kid, another on the way.

She married . . . a Spanish *poet*.

He grimaces.

She translated his work and fell in love with him.

Fell in love with a collection of poems.

They were called . . . '*Solitude*'.

He holds on to the flowers.

I have to put these at Blackfriars Bridge.

Dan *and* **Anna** *stand*.

I have to go, I'll miss the plane.

They look at each other.

Goodbye.

Anna   Yes. Goodbye.

They exit separately.

Empty stage.

Blackout.

Appendix to Scene Three

In a production of *Closer* where budget or theatre sightlines won't allow for a projected version of this scene it may be possible for the actors to speak their lines whilst 'typing'. Permission, in this respect, must be sought from the author's agent when applying for the rights for the production.

The following dialogue may be used:

Scene Three

Early evening. January (the following year).

Dan *is in his flat sitting at a table with a computer.*
There is a Newton's Cradle on the table. Writerly sloth, etc.

Larry *is sitting at his hospital desk with a computer.*
He is wearing a white coat.

They are in separate rooms.

They speak their 'dialogue' simultaneous to their typing it.
*The actors should speak word by word, almost robotically, as if they were dictating the words on to the screen, thus making a distinction between 'typed' speech and 'spoken' speech (e.g. **Larry** on the phone).*

Dan   Hallo.

Larry   Hi.

Dan   How are you?

Larry   OK.

Dan   Cum here often?

Larry   First time.

Dan   A Virgin. Welcome. What's your name?

Larry   Larry. You?

Dan *considers.*

Dan   Anna.

Larry   Nice to meet you.

Dan   I love COCK.

Pause.

Larry   You're v. forward.

Dan   And you are chatting on 'LONDON FUCK'. Do you want sex?

Larry   Yes. Describe you.

Dan   Dark hair. Dirty mouth. Epic Tits.

Larry   Define Epic.

Dan   Thirty-six double D.

Larry   Nice arse?

Dan   Y.

Larry   Because I want to know.

Dan *smiles.*

Dan   No, 'Y' means 'Yes'.

Larry   Oh.

Dan   I want to suck you senseless.

Larry   Be my guest.

Dan   Sit on my face, Fuckboy.

Larry   I'm there.

Dan   Wear my wet knickers.

Beat.

Larry   OK.

Dan   Are you well hung?

Larry   Nine pounds.

Larry (*speaking*)   Shit.

Larry (*typing*)   Nine inches.

Dan   GET IT OUT.

Larry *considers and then unzips. He puts his hand in his trousers. The phone on his desk rings. Loud. He jumps.*

Larry (*speaking*)   Wait.

Larry (*typing*)   wait.

Larry *picks up the phone.* **Dan** *lights a cigarette.*

Larry (*speaking*)   <u>Yes</u>. What's the histology? *Progressive?* Sounds like an atrophy.

Larry *puts the phone down and goes back to his keyboard.* **Dan** *clicks the balls on his Newton's Cradle.*

Larry   Hallo?

Dan *looks at his screen.*

Larry   Anna.

Larry (*speaking*)   Bollocks.

Larry (*typing*)   ANNA? WHERE ARE YOU?

Dan   Hey, big Larry, what do you wank about?

Larry *considers.*

Larry   Ex-girlfriends.

Dan   Not current g-friends?

Larry   Never.

Dan *smiles.*

Dan   Tell me your sex-ex fantasy . . .

Larry   Hotel room . . . they tie me up . . . tease me . . . won't let me come. They fight over me, six tongues on my cock, balls, perineum, et cetera.

Dan   All hail the Sultan of Twat?

Larry *laughs.*

Larry   Anna, what do you wank about?

Dan *thinks.*

Dan   Strangers.

Larry   Details.

Dan   They form a queue and I attend to them like a cum hungry bitch, one in each hole and both hands.

Larry   Then?

Dan   They come in my mouth arse tits cunt hair.

Larry (*speaking*)   Jesus.

Larry's *phone rings. He picks up the receiver and replaces it without answering. Then he takes it off the hook.*

Larry (*typing*)   Then?

Dan   I lick it off like the dirty slut I am. Wait, have to type with one hand . . . I'm coming right now . . . oh oh oh oh oh oh oh oh oh oh oh oh oh oh oh.

Pause. **Larry***, motionless, stares at his screen.*

Larry   Was it good?

Dan   No.

Larry *shakes his head.*

Larry   I'm shocked.

Dan   PARADISE SHOULD BE SHOCKING.

Larry   Are you for real?

Beat.

Dan   MEET ME.

Pause.

Larry   Serious?

Dan   Yes.

Larry   When.

Dan   NOW.

Larry   Can't. I'm a doctor. Must do rounds.

Dan *smiles.* **Larry** *flicks through his desk diary.*

Dan   Don't be a pussy. Life without risk is death. Desire, like the world, is an accident. The best sex is anonymous. We live as we dream, ALONE. I'll make you come like a train.

Larry   Tomorrow, one p.m., where?

Dan *thinks.*

Dan   The Aquarium, London Zoo, and then HOTEL.

Larry   How will you know me?

Dan   Bring white coat.

Larry   Eh?

Dan   Doctor plus coat equals horn for me.

Larry   OK.

Dan   I send you a rose my love.

Larry   Thanks. See you at Aquarium. Bye, Anna.

Dan   Bye, Larry, kiss kiss kiss kiss kiss.

Larry   Kiss kiss kiss kiss kiss kiss.

They look at their screens.

Blackout.